W9-AAI-034

GOD'S COVENANT
WITH ISRAEL

ESTABLISHING BIBLICAL BOUNDARIES
IN TODAY'S WORLD

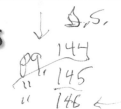

Balfour Books

A Division of New Leaf Publishing Group

First printing: July 2005

Copyright © 2005 by Binyamin Elon. All rights reserved. No part of this book may be used or reproduced in any manner whatsoever without written permission of the publisher, except in the case of brief quotations in articles and reviews. For information write New Leaf Press, P.O. Box 726, Green Forest, AR 72638.

ISBN: 0-89221-627-1
Library of Congress Control Number: 2005929856

Editors: Dr. Larry Keefauver and Rebekah Casey
Project Coordinator: Stuart Schnee
Cover design: Left Coast Design, Portland, OR
Design: Shilo/Barkats, Beth El, Brent Spurlock

All biblical quotes unless otherwise noted are from the New King James Version. Copyright ©1979, 1980 & 1982 by Thomas Nelson, Inc. Used by permission. All rights reserved.

Printed in the United States of America

Please visit our website for other great titles:
www.balfourbooks.net

For information regarding author interviews,
please contact the publicity department at (870) 438-5288.

Balfour Books

A Division of New Leaf Publishing Group

TABLE OF CONTENTS

Chapter 5

Chapter 6

FOREWORD

A wise man once said "A friend in need is a friend indeed." I learned this lesson in one of the most difficult times for my people and myself personally. My colleague, retired I.D.F. General Rehavam Ze'evi, was the Minister of Tourism when he was assassinated in a Jerusalem hotel in November of 2001. It was under these devastating circumstances that I assumed the position of Minister of Tourism in Israel.

This was a very bad time in Israel. The city centers had been abandoned, and the people of Israel found themselves victims of a terrorist war against the civilian population. The tourism industry was completely depleted, which resulted in a badly damaged economy. Every facet of life in Israel was so difficult in this time. Our spirits were broken, our streets were empty, and our very existence was threatened.

I met with my staff and ordered an immediate redirection of our marketing campaigns. Rather than publishing full-page ads and overpriced articles in prestigious magazines, I directed them to begin a direct marketing campaign. We began to knock on the doors of churches and

synagogues. Many people accepted this personal invitation and came to Israel.

Those who came in spite of the situation saved the Israeli tourism industry. They brought light to the once darkened streets of Jerusalem and warmth to our hearts. Hundreds of thousands of people arrived, group after group. They came and brought us hope.

I will never forget the Feast of Tabernacles when thousands of Christians marched in the streets of Jerusalem. Shopkeepers who had been struggling to stay in business were amazed at this sight. They asked the Christian pilgrims how they had the courage to come to Israel in such a difficult time. The visitors responded that they came to Jerusalem for the Feast of Tabernacles in fulfillment of the prophecy spoken by Zachariah (14:16). They also said that they refused to allow evil, specifically in the form of terrorism, to separate them from Israel.

I learned to appreciate the deep kinship between Christians and the people of Israel. In order to maintain this friendship, I decided to open my heart and share with you the challenges that I face in Israel.

I believe that if you do not know how to read the Bible, you cannot understand the daily newspaper. If you do not know the Biblical story of Abraham, Isaac, and Jacob (who became Israel), you cannot possibly understand the miracle of the modern State of Israel.

I would like to leave you with a few closing thoughts:
    Israel Is Real!
    The word of God Is Real!
    The covenant between God and Israel Is Real!
    The State of Israel Is Real!

Rabbi Binyamin Elon

INTRODUCTION

WE'RE HOME!

The Jewish people are back! We have come home!

The most significant historic drama of our age is taking place in front of our incredulous eyes. The Jews were thrown into a long exile two millennia ago. We are now re-gathering in our historic home-land, the land of our holy destiny.

It is evident everywhere: from the "children play-ing in the streets of Jerusalem"[1] to the long-famil-iar rolling hills of Judea and Samaria, and in the rainbow of colors and customs of the myriads of Jews arriving in Israel from all over the world.

After nineteen centuries of exile, masses of Jews began returning to their Promised Land. We had been exiled for our sins, but we never forgot our homeland. We have always prayed for the chance to return to Jerusalem.

My father's family is a testament to this yearning. Immediately upon Hitler's rise to power, they understood what was about to befall the Jews of Europe. They left their birthplace in Germany for Palestine. I remember that as a child I was among the few students in my school whose grandparents did not perish in the Holocaust.

My father, Menachem Elon, came to Palestine in 1935 and went on to become Israel's Deputy Supreme Court Justice. My mother's family lived in Israel for generations. She gave me the rare honor of being the seventh generation of her family to be born in Israel.

Today, I reflect on my family history and the arduous paths that they chiseled through their exile. The Diaspora left the children of Israel far from the Promised Land, far from any independent state with Jewish sovereignty and far from the Hebrew language. There is no rational explanation for the miracle of the return of the Jewish people from every corner of the world to the Land of Israel. Only one who reads and believes the Bible can begin to understand this miracle.

I have been serving as a member of the Knesset (Israel's parliament) for the past nine years. It is not always easy to converse with those of my parliamentary colleagues, who do not understand the meaning of the Bible. Some of them have disparagingly called me a "fundamentalist" — to differentiate from those liberals who let only pragmatic security and strategic considerations guide them. There is no insult of which I am more proud.

I do not believe that any building without a biblical and divine foundation can stand today in this place and at this time. As it says in Psalm 127:1

"Unless the Lord builds the house,
They labor in vain who build it."

I walk the streets of the Promised Land where Abraham walked. I drive through the roads and plains where Isaac tended his flocks. I hike to the hilltops from where Jacob peered expectantly in all directions — *"Towards the sea, and eastward, and northward, and towards the South."*[2] I see these things and remember clearly the Biblical truth: God gave the Promised Land, all of it, to our Patriarchs: Abraham, Isaac and Jacob.

It is wondrous to live in Israel at this time in history, knowing that our forefathers paved the way for this very time. Their love of the land was evident in everything they did. For one thing, they were constantly traveling in Israel, as if they could never get enough of it. Abraham was commanded to do so by God: *"Arise, walk in the land through its length and its width, for I give it to you."*[3]

Abraham and his descendants traveled the land and built altars upon it to give thanks to God. This was one of the ways in which they showed their closeness to the Creator. The Bible conscientiously recounts the locations of the altars that Abraham built.

2. Genesis 28:14.
3. Genesis 13:17.

Shechem

The four altars that established the covenant connection between God, Abraham and the Land of Israel.
1. **Shechem**
2. **Beth El**
3. **Hebron**
4. **Jerusalem**

Abraham's son, Isaac, and his grandson, Jacob, built altars in Beersheba. Jacob built two more altars, in Shechem and in Beth El. The signs of the attachment of our Patriarchs to God were thus apparent all over the land.

The continual attacks against Israel are attacks against our Biblical roots. These roots confirm

God's covenant with Abraham, Isaac, Jacob, and all their descendants to occupy and possess the land.

The Bible states that our forefathers purchased three sites. It records that they paid "hard cash" to the people who lived there. These places are Hebron, Shechem, and Jerusalem.

Abraham purchased Hebron as a burial place for his wife Sarah.[4] Jacob purchased the field of Shechem "for 100 kesitah"[5] and Jerusalem was purchased by King David from the Jebusites.[6] These are the three cities at the heart of the conflict in Israel today.

Beth El

4. Genesis 23.
5. Genesis 33:19.
6. I Chronicles 21:24–25.

Hebron: Tomb of the Patriarchs.

I believe that we cannot deal with this conflict without exploring God's covenant with the land and its meaning for all those we affectionately call the "People of the Book." Christians and Jews who take God at His word in Scripture, and believe wholeheartedly that God's covenant with Israel is everlasting, have a responsibility to know, understand, and honor that covenant.

Jerusalem: The Western Wall.

CHAPTER ONE

A Momentous Time in History

The Four Pillars of God's Covenant with Israel

The connection between the four altars and the sites purchased by Abraham, Jacob, and King David give us historical and Biblical roots for understanding God's covenant with the children of Israel for the Land of Israel.

Tom Hess, a long-time friend of Israel and a Christian resident of Jerusalem, effectively noted these Biblical roots and how they relate to modern history. In his book, *God's Abrahamic Covenants with Israel,* Tom writes that the enemies of Israel are: "trying to destroy the foundations and knock down the pillars of the House of Israel, and cause the Jewish people to break covenants with their God in the very places where God made covenants with

His people... The four places where Abraham built altars are in the very center of Israel, the very center of the land where those who do not believe in the God of Israel and His covenants say should be an Islamic Palestinian state." [7]

The Four Altars and Their Impact Today

Let us consider how the four altars are significantly linked to what is happening in Israel today.

Altar 1 — Shechem. The first altar was located in Shechem. This was the first site in the Land of Israel where God revealed himself to Abraham: *"Abram passed through the land to the place of Shechem, as far as the terebinth tree of Moreh. And the Canaanites were then in the land. Then the Lord appeared to Abram and said, 'To your descendants I will give this land.'"* [8] Abraham built an altar in Shechem and God consecrated the covenant.

The Arabs of Israel know Shechem as Nablus, an Arabic corruption of Flavia Neopolis, the name given to it by the Romans. This city is known for the holy tomb of Joseph. It is actually the place where Joseph and his sons Menashe and Ephraim were buried. It is now in a shocking state of destruction and desecration.

7. Tom Hess. "God's Abrahamic Covenant with Israel- Biblical Road Map of Reconciliation. Restoring the Altars, Foundations, Pillars and Mountains of Israel." Progressive Vision International, 2004.
8. Genesis 12: 6,7.

Whatever the political ramifications of the sacrilege of Joseph's Tomb, the fact is that it occurred at the site of the altar of Abraham and Jacob. The defilement of this site is an attempt to desecrate God's promise to Israel.

Those who believe in the Bible must ask themselves how we allowed a site so significant to our heritage to be abandoned and desecrated. The Jews are the children of Abraham and the Christians are children of Abraham by faith. Together we must accept guardianship over the places that symbolize the foundations of our faith.

Altar 2 — Beth El. Abraham built the second altar, in Beth El.[9] God verified the covenant over His seed and over the land in Jacob's dream. *"And behold, the Lord stood above it and said: 'I am the Lord God of Abraham your father and the God of Isaac; the land on which you lie I will give to you and your descendants.'"*[10] Beth El is also the place where God informed Jacob that his name would become Israel.

Beth El is replete with milestones in the history of God and Israel, but biblical history records some negative things about Beth El as well. King Jeroboam built a golden calf and an altar for idol worship there.[11]

Beth El is located adjacent to the Arab city of Ramallah, the place that arch-terrorist Yasser Arafat chose to be the capital of the Palestinian Authority.

9. Genesis 12: 8, 13: 4.
10. Genesis 28:13.
11. I Kings 12.

Arafat tried to rebuild an altar to Baal in Ramallah. This was an attempt to adopt a Canaanite identity in order to prove that Muslim claims to Israel preceded the Jewish connections to Israel. In 1998, the Palestinian Authority issued a postal stamp with the name and image of Baal on it.[12]

Baal
Canaan's Painting
بعل رسم كنعاني

Altar 3 — Hebron. Abraham built the third altar in Hebron after he separated from his nephew Lot. Here God reconfirmed His covenant with Abraham, his offspring, and the land. *"For all the land which you see I give to you and your descendants forever. And I will make your descendants as the dust of the earth; so that if a man could number the dust of the earth, then your descendants also could be numbered. Arise, walk in the land through its length and its width, for I give it to you. Then Abram moved his tent, and went and dwelt by the terebinth trees of Mamre, which are in Hebron, and built an altar there to the Lord."* [13]

12. Cultural Institute of the Italian Islamic Community. "A Fatwa of Dissociation from those who Honor Baal." January 12, 2005. **http://members.xoom.virgilio.it/_XOOM/amislam/baal.html**. This stamp can also be found at: The Palestinian Stamp Gallery. **http://www.palestine-mail.com/ stamps/canaan.html**.
13. Genesis 13:15-18.

Hebron is the City of the Patriarchs. Abraham purchased the land in Hebron.[14] Abraham,[15] Sarah,[16] Isaac,[17] Rebekah,[18] Jacob,[19] and Leah[20] were buried in Hebron. King David ruled from Hebron for seven years and according to the Jewish sages, Caleb prayed for guidance in Hebron.[21]

The legacy of Hebron has been under attack by radical Islam in an attempt to break a physical link in the chain connecting God and Israel. The Jews of Hebron were forced to flee this holy city in 1929 after an Arab pogrom took the lives of 76 innocent Jewish residents. Jews returned to Hebron in 1967 despite many horrific attempts to drive them out. Dozens of Jews have been brutally murdered in Hebron in the midst of vicious attacks targeted at innocent civilians. We must encourage Jews to continue to live in Hebron and protect the burial site of our Patriarchs and Matriarchs as well as the site where Abraham built the third altar to symbolize his covenant with God.

14. Genesis 23:2-9.
15. Genesis 25:10.
16. Genesis 23:19.
17. Genesis 35:29;49:31.
18. Genesis 49:31.
19. Genesis 49:29.
20. Genesis 49:31.
21. The Babylonian Talmud, Tractate Sota, p34 B

The Quest for Jerusalem.

Altar 4 — Jerusalem. Modern history of the conflict in Israel has shown that radical Islam has zeroed in on the sites fundamental to the covenant between God and Israel. Undermining sites that express the covenant between God and Israel is an expression of opposition to God. This is blatantly illustrated in the fourth of Abraham's chosen locations: Jerusalem.

Mt. Moriah is situated in Jerusalem. This is the place where Abraham was willing to offer up his son Isaac,[22] and where the Temple Mount, Judaism's most deeply sacred site, still stands. It is written in II Chronicles 3:1. *"Now Solomon began to build the house of the Lord at Jerusalem on Mount Moriah, where the Lord had appeared to his father David, at the place that David had prepared on the threshing floor of Ornan the Jebusite."*

22. Genesis 22:2.

"Their backs were toward (the place of) the temple of the Lord, and their faces toward the east."
Ezekiel 8:16

Muslims pray with their backs to Jerusalem, but it is toward this holy site that the Arab world is directing all of its militant and political efforts.

It is difficult to grasp the full meaning of radical Islam's military and political struggle against Jerusalem. The religious war against the significance of Jerusalem to the Jews and Christians is also difficult to understand. The jihad against the God-Israel connection begins with Isaac, the son whose binding on Mt. Moriah symbolized the depth of the relationship between God and Abraham.

Islam states that it was not Isaac who was chosen to continue the Abrahamic line, but rather Ishmael. This is in complete contrast to the Bible. God told Abraham, *"And as for Ishmael, I have heard thee: Behold, I have blessed him and will make him fruitful, and will multiply him exceedingly; twelve princes shall he beget, and I will make him a great nation. But my covenant will I establish with Isaac."* [23] Later on God told Abraham not to grieve over the casting out of Ishmael, *"for in Isaac your seed shall be called."* [24]

Islam identifies Ishmael as one of the prophets, although the Koranic description of the binding by Abraham does not identify Ishmael as the one to be sacrificed.[25] After arguments between Islamic sages regarding the binding, the opinion was accepted that Ishmael was the one to be sacrificed by Abraham. Islamic sages later accused the Jews of purposely concealing the fact that Ishmael was the one to be sacrificed.[26] The Koran asserts that Abraham and Ishmael built the Kaaba,[27] the black stone

---

23. Genesis 17:20-21.
24. Genesis 21:12.
25. The Koran. Penguin Classics Version. Middlesex; Penguin Books Ltd., 1956. Sura 37:102 (p.172).
26. GIBB, H.A.R. and KRAMERS, J.H. "Shorter Encyclopedia of Islam." London: Luzac & Co. 1961 (p.179).

located in Mecca, which pre-existed Islam. Muslims pray toward Mecca, the holiest site of Islam.

Islam was born as a rebellion against the covenant of the God of Israel. For one to believe in the God of Israel, one must admit that the Biblical covenant continued from Abraham to Isaac and Isaac to Jacob, whose name was changed to Israel. Islamic theology maintains that Allah made a covenant which progressed through Ishmael.

Islam was founded more than 600 years after the birth of Christianity, and thousands of years after God gave the Torah to Moses. As a result, Islamic scholars have made great efforts to recreate history to fit Islamic theology. Islamic revisionist history has set out to prove that all the holy sites of Judaism and Christianity rightfully belong to Islam.

Islamic scholars claim that Islam views Moses and Jesus as prophets, and thus it is a tolerant and perfect religion. Anyone who learns even a little history knows that Islam is a religion of force, broken treaties, and war. This has long been evidenced from the first peace treaty of Islam, to the massacre of Christians and Jews in 7th Century Palestine and later, the decimation of Christian and Jewish holy sites in Jerusalem. The campaign to place mosques on the Temple Mount and atop Christian holy sites is intended to prove that Islam is superior to all other religions.

27. Sura 2:127 (p. 345).

After the horrific tragedy of September 11, 2001, the recurring theme was that Islam is a religion of peace. Islamic clerics gave interviews stating that Islam accepts Moses and Jesus as prophets, therefore they peacefully accept Christianity and Judaism. It is true that Islam accepts Jesus as a prophet, but this general statement is a slippery slope.

According to Islamic theology Jesus is a prophet of Islam who will return at the end of days. Muslims believe that after his return, Jesus will pray behind the Imam (in submission) and break the cross. They believe that Jesus will decimate churches and synagogues, kill all Christians, and be buried by the side of Muhammad in Medina.[28]

We have seen that Islam may superficially accept Christianity and Judaism, but Islamic intellectuals say that our Bible is full of lies and the Koran is the true version of God's word. Islamic revisionist historians have attempted to recreate history, using parts of the Bible to support their claim. Islam did not suffice with merely changing the written historical record. It sought to change the facts on the ground by altering archaeological records to fit Islamic theology.

28. Shorter Encyclopedia of Islam (p. 174).

The Systematic Destruction of the Temple Mount by Islamic Leaders

Soon after the creation of the Palestinian Authority in 1993, the Muslim Waqf — the body charged with supervising the Temple Mount — began overseeing a series of excavations and construction works on the holy site. This project had two goals:

- To erase all traces of Jewish history on the Mount:
  "They merely want to cover up all signs of Jewish history there." [29]
- To turn it into an Arab-Moslem site, with mosques all over the compound.

In 1996, the Waqf ignored the status quo that had been observed for generations. Two ancient underground Second Temple Period structures were converted into a new large mosque on the Temple Mount. The new mosque extends over an area of 1.5 acres. It is the largest mosque in Israel, able to accommodate 10,000 people.

In November 1999, Islamic clerics opened what they called an "emergency exit" to the new mosque. It actually became a gigantic hole, 18,000 square feet in size, and almost 36 feet deep.

29. Dr. Eilat Mazar, of the Committee for the Prevention of the Destruction of Antiquities, in March 2004 (**www.israelnationalnews.com/news.php3?id=59262**).

Stones that Archeologists have dated to the Second Temple Period.

As a result of the digging, thousands of tons of ancient artifacts from as early as the First Temple Period were unceremoniously dumped into the Kidron Valley. In subsequent construction/destruction work, another ancient underground Second Temple Period structure was converted into a mosque. As a result, bulldozers destroyed an ancient arched structure against the Eastern Wall of the Temple Mount enclosure.

In January of 2002, Islamic Movement leader Israeli-Arab Sheikh Raed Salah told reporters that the "use of the Temple Mount is exclusively a Moslem Arab Palestinian right." He denied any Jewish rights on the Mount claiming, "There never was any First or Second Temple in the vicinity of the Mosque." [30] More than once I have heard Arab members of Knesset state that the Temple Mount is "Haram al Sharif," and deny that either the First or Second Temples ever existed.

Rabbi Chaim Richman of the Temple Mount Institute in Jerusalem wrote of the attempt to erase Jewish history from the Temple Mount:

> The stones themselves [that have been destroyed] are not even the issue! For as painful as it is to see the remnants of the House of the Lord treated like rubbish, and to know that it is all part of an effort to erase Jewish history from the annals of Jerusalem...still, we know that one day the Holy Temple will be rebuilt, from new stones, and it will not be destroyed. *"The glory of the last house will be greater than that of the former, and in this place I shall grant peace,"* [31] God tells us through the prophet Haggai...

Rabbi Richman writes that in the course of filming the destruction:

> We were accosted by [Arab] residents of the area who were angered by our presence, and who were made very uncomfortable by our intense interest in this "rubble." One man angrily approached us and told us "This is my land. You have no business being here. You come here to make trouble about nothing. You Jews are coming here and crying, but there is nothing

30. "More Moslem Plans To Destroy Jewish Bonds With The Temple Mount" Arutz Sheva August 20,2004 **http://www.israelnn.com/news.php3?id=67671**.
31. Haggai 2:9

of yours here. These rocks...there is nothing of yours here; get out...these rocks are nothing to you, nothing...all over the world, the Jews make all the trouble."

Nothing has changed. We were reminded of the following words from the book of Nehemiah...what a chilling "coincidence!": *"But it came to pass, that when Sanvallat heard that we were building the wall, he was angry, and greatly enraged, and he mocked the Jews. And he said... What are these feeble Jews doing? Will they restore things? Will they sacrifice? Will they make an end in a day? Will they revive the stones out of the heaps of the rubbish, seeing they are burned?"* [32]

For 2,000 years we have faced challenges and overcome them. We have heard these words before — "Will they revive the stones?"; "There is nothing of yours here;" "Jerusalem has always been an Islamic city;" "there never was any Temple on the Temple Mount..." We have faced challenges, and we have overcome them all. Yes, we shall revive the stones out of the heaps of rubbish. [33]

During the past several years public opinion within Israel galvanized to demand a cessation of the destruction on the Temple Mount. Urgent letters were sent to the Prime Minister and cabinet ministers, warning of "a serious act of irreparable vandalism and destruction carried out without supervision, while abrogating the law."

32. Nehemiah 4:1–2.
33. Rabbi Chaim Richman. "Reviving the Stones." Light to the Nations 2002
   http://www.lttn.org/00-01-02-email.html.

An open letter about the destruction was sent to the Prime Minister. Numerous highly respected Israeli individuals, including former Jerusalem mayors Teddy Kollek and Ehud Olmert, authors Amos Oz and Haim Gouri, and 82 members of Israel's Knesset signed the letter. It should not be surprising that they were appalled that the law requiring the preservation of all holy places was brazenly ignored on the Temple Mount, the most holy place to more people than any other site around the world.

The destruction of antiquities on the Temple Mount goes hand in hand with Israeli policy illegally preventing the press from visiting the area. Former and current security officials dispute the claim that "security concerns" require Israeli indulgence on the Temple Mount. This sacred place is being demolished while Israeli authorities and the world indifferently stand by.

The Committee for the Prevention of the Destruction of Antiquities on the Temple Mount, founded in January 2000, is an apolitical volunteer group, made up of well-known Israeli public figures, including archaeologists, writers, lawyers, justices, and members of the Security Services. The committee was formed in order to preserve the antiquities on the Temple Mount regardless of political, national, or religious affiliation.

The committee demands that the Israeli government:

- Stop the destruction on the Temple Mount.
- Open the Temple Mount to Israeli and international media.
- Enable the Antiquities Authority to fulfill its duties and guard the antiquities in the State of Israel.
- See that the status quo on the Temple Mount is preserved and ensure that all changes should be deeply considered and undertaken in a way that would not destroy ancient remains.

Construction continues to destroy the ancient structures of the Temple Mount. Tractors are digging and dumping artifacts without any archaeological supervision. A large stone saw constantly cuts into our heritage, destroying dozens of ancient stones into slabs used for the new paving and construction on the Temple Mount.

Unbelievable stories flow from Arab sources contending that Jewish people have no ancient connection to the site. Arab treatment of the Temple Mount excavations seeks to hide the evidence. All experts agree that great care should be exercised when excavating the Temple area. Trained archaeologists should be in charge. Skilled students of history should enhance our knowledge of Jewish, Muslim, and Christian history through new discoveries at this holy place.

Ancient pillars, crowns and rocks that were removed from the Temple Mount.

Special hand tools should be used to protect each sliver of the ancient world. Surgical precision is demanded in ancient excavations. Sand must be sifted, shards of clay dusted, and relics protectively guarded.

But this is not the practice at the Arab-controlled portion of the Temple Mount. Instead, our holy mountain is being "excavated" with Arab bulldozers by Palestinian heavy equipment operators. Agenda-driven Arab leaders are attempting to erase Jewish history from the Temple Mount. In a futile effort to cover the past, historical artifacts are destroyed as Arabs bury the truth in an attempt to prop up false claims of ownership. It is a travesty. Christians and Jews should raise an outcry. Someone must sound the alarm on the Temple Mount! Who will stop this destruction? Who will prohibit the erasure of religious history? Arab propagandists must stop destroying vestiges of ancient life from the site.

It is imperative that Christians recognize the evil intent behind this behavior. It is a classical revision of history. The Arab press shamelessly spews rhetoric declaring that even the Nazi Holocaust never happened! It is reassuring that the most vehement Arab activist cannot change the truth. In the 1930's, their own Supreme Muslim Council declared the Temple Mount "beyond dispute" as the location of Solomon's Temple![34]

U.S. Congressman Eric Cantor (R-Va.) introduced a bill in the House of Representatives on July 19, 2001, entitled "The Temple Mount Preservation Act of 2001" (HR 2566). It called for the suspension of U.S. aid as long as the PA continues its construction/destruction works on the Temple Mount.

Although this bill has languished in the International Relations Committee, it makes some important statements about the situation on the Temple Mount. Details of the brutal destruction of the Temple Mount by the Muslims are clearly laid out, beginning with the conversion of two ancient underground Second Temple Period structures,

34. Dr. Randy Weiss. "Who Owns Jerusalem's Temple Mount?" October, 2005
   www.crosstalk.org/articles/mount.shtml.

Solomon's Stables, and the Western Hulda Gate, into a new mosque. The bill continues to recount recent Temple Mount history:

> In early 1998, the Waqf, controlled by the Palestinian Authority, began further excavation. A major underground mosque hall was inaugurated in August 1999 and an emergency exit was opened to a mosque located on the Temple Mount. The exit is 18,000 square feet in size and up to 36 feet deep, and thousands of tons of ancient fills from the site were dumped into the Kidron Valley. Archeologists have subsequently determined that artifacts dumped into the Kidron Valley from the Temple Mount dated from the period of the First Temple (circa 1006 B.C.E) to 586 B.C.E.

> In mid-2000, Arafat deployed onto the Temple Mount armed and unarmed security personnel of Jibril Rajoub's Preventive Security Forces in violation of numerous past agreements with Israel. Rajoub's forces evicted the Waqf's personnel and consolidated Arafat's control and ability to wage the Intifada ("uprising") against Israel (which started at the end of September, 2000 when Ariel Sharon, as head of the opposition visited the Temple Mount). The Arabs called this revolt "El-Aksa," referring to their mosque at the Temple Mount that they felt was violated by Sharon's visit.

In February and March of 2001, bulldozers razed an ancient arched structure built against the Eastern Wall of the Temple Mount enclosure in order to further enlarge the emergency gate of the new mosque at the Stables of Solomon.

In early May, Arafat ordered that the underground halls under the Temple Mount be unified into a single fortified space that would be both the largest mosque ever built on Haram al-Sharif [the Temple Mount] and a springboard for the forthcoming Palestinian struggle for control of the Temple Mount. Given the haste and unsupervised nature of the ongoing excavation and construction work, there is great fear that the foundations of the two Holy Mosques will be severely damaged to the point of collapse.

The actions of Yasser Arafat and the Palestinian Authority threaten to eliminate all historical evidence of Jewish activity on the Temple Mount and serve to discredit Israeli claims of sovereignty over the Temple Mount.

The massive excavation and unsupervised destruction of artifacts discovered within the Temple Mount are undeniable affronts to the concepts of religious freedom and tolerance that must be respected in order to achieve and maintain peace in the Middle East. The destruction of the Temple Mount, which threatens to incite more violence, is destroying sacred artifacts and jeopardizing the ability of Americans to understand and promote their Judeo-Christian heritage.[35]

It is devastating that bulldozers ruthlessly dug up relics of Jewish history. Archaeological evidence of our historic, religious, and national connection to Mt. Moriah was carted away in truckloads to a desolate wadi behind Jerusalem. The ancient stones and pillars that were not discarded were cut into new shapes, to be used to pave the "new" Temple Mount.

Please visit www.har-habayt.org on the Internet, to learn how this shocking desecration was perpetrated.

Islam and the Christian World

It is critically important to understand Islamic theology as it pertains to Christianity. Islamic religious wars are not restricted to the Jews alone. Muslim end of days theology places Muslims juxtaposed to the "People of the Book," and Muslims believe that both the Jews and the Christians will be wiped out entirely. "First the Jews on the Sabbath, then the Christians on Sunday" is a commonly known summary of their belief.

35. "The Temple Mount Preservation Act of 2001"
(HR2566) **http://thomas.loc.gov/cgi-bin/bdquery/z?d107:HR02566:@@@L&summ2=m&**.

Muslim author Dr. Shamim A. Siddiqi of New York, has identified the U.S. government and Christianity as Islam's greatest enemies. He formulated this issue quite well in a letter to New York Post columnist Dr. Daniel Pipes:

> "Abraham, Moses, Jesus, and Muhammad were all prophets of Islam," Siddiqi wrote. "Islam is the common heritage of the Judeo-Christian-Muslim community of America... Islam was the din [faith, way of life] of both Jews and Christians, who later lost it through human innovations. Now the Muslims want to remind their Jewish and Christian brothers and sisters of their original din. These are the facts of history." [36]

Dr. Mark Durie provides a fascinating analysis:

> This historical negationism — appearing to affirm Christianity and Judaism whilst in fact rejecting and supplanting them — is a lynch pin of Muslim apologetics. What is being affirmed is in fact neither Christianity nor Judaism, but Jesus as a prophet of Islam and Moses as a Muslim. This is intended to lead to "reversion" of Christians and Jews to Islam, which is what Siddiqi refers to when he speaks of "the joint responsibility" of Jews and Christians to establish "the Kingdom of God". By this he means that American Christians and Jews should work to establish shari'ah law and the rule of Islam in the United States. [37]

---

36. Daniel Pipes. "The Danger Within: Militant Islam in America." Commentary Magazine Vol. 113, February 2002. **http://www.meforum.org/article/pipes/117**.
37. Dr. Mark Durie. "Islamic Jesus." January 12, 2005.
   http://answering-islam.org.uk/Intro/Islamic_jesus.html.

Such superficial acceptance of Judaism and Christianity, while maintaining an underlying rejection of both, is part of the Islamic strategy to undermine support of Israel. Radical Islam is not waiting to annihilate the Jews before clashing with Christians. Christians have been massacred in dozens of terrorist acts and hostile clashes around the world.

On March 3, 2000, then U.S. Senator Connie Mack told the Senate about his visit to Israel:

> Periodically, there are incidents of Christian-Muslim tension in the occupied territories. Tensions have arisen over Christian-Muslim romantic relationships or when Christians have erected large crosses in the public domain. Christians in the Bethlehem area also have complained about Muslims settling there and constructing homes illegally on land not zoned for building.
>
> During the period covered by this report, there were periodic reports that some Christian converts from Islam who publicize their religious beliefs have been harassed. Converts complained that they were mistreated and threatened. The draft Palestinian Basic Law specifically forbids discrimination against individuals based on their religion; however, the PA did not take any action against persons accused of harassment.[38]

---

38. Senator Connie Mack, Speech U.S. Senate, March 3, 2000.

Many other incidents show the Palestinian Authority's brutality towards Christians:

- In 1976, the Palestinian Liberation Organization massacred 586 Lebanese Christians in Damor.
- In 1997, the Russian Orthodox Church in Hebron was taken over by the PLO. PA paramilitary police burst into a monastery, and they beat and dragged out monks and nuns. Several nuns and monks required hospitalization.
- In January 2000, the Palestinian Authority forcefully took over the 19th century Russian Orthodox Church in Jericho.
- In Nazareth, Jesus' hometown, radical Islamic militants nearly caused a small battle because they started building, in violation of governmental decisions, a giant mosque on Christian-owned land.
- In April of 2002, 200 Palestinian terrorists seized the Church of the Nativity in Bethlehem. 60 monks, nuns, and priests were held hostage during the standoff.
- Two American courts granted asylum to Palestinian Christian Arabs, on the grounds that they would be persecuted for their religious beliefs if they return to PA-controlled territory.
- The U.S. State Department's Religious Freedom Report in 2000 detailed the harassment of Christians in PLO areas and illegal construction on property owned by Christians.[39]

39. 2000 Annual Report on International Religious Freedom. Released by the Bureau of Democracy, Human Rights, and Labor. U.S. Department of State, September 5, 2000. **http://www.state.gov/www/global/human_rights/irf/irf_rpt/irf_occterr.html**.

These are just a few of the atrocities that have been committed against Christians in PLO areas.

Ramallah, Bethlehem, Lebanon, and the Christian Quarter in Jerusalem were at one time predominantly Christian areas. Radical Islam intimidated and attacked the Christians to such an extent that these areas are now becoming almost Christian-free.

The Bottom Line

The children of Israel have come home to Zion in fulfillment of the covenant. There are some who are desperately fighting God's plan for history. They have pinpointed the most sensitive points of the God-Israel relationship, and that is where they are concentrating their efforts.

The Jewish people are living a model national life in their God-promised land, while their enemies — and those of God — are either vanquished or accept the goodness Israel brings to the world.

CHAPTER TWO

A Permanent Inheritance . . . Until this very Day

In 1823, my mother's great-grandmother came to Hebron with a Lubavitch group from Russia. They came to the land under harsh conditions in order to strengthen and provide support to the Jewish community in Hebron. I would like to share with you a special commentary by the last great Rabbi of the Lubavitch movement, a movement which holds a special place in my heart.[40]

The Lubavitch Rabbi, Menachem Mendel Schneerson, wrote a commentary[41] in which he expounded on the writings of the Jewish sages and Biblical passages. Regarding the altars, he wrote that each of the altars has a unique and spiritual meaning, a significance that symbolizes another level of connection between Israel and the land.

40. Sue Fishcoff. "The Rebbe's Army Inside the World of Chabad Lubavitch." New York: Random House, 2003.
41. Rabbi Menacham Mendel Schneerson. Sichat: 7 Chesvan 5746, New York: Chabad.

Abraham journeyed throughout his life and throughout the Land of Israel. Even after establishing the covenant and building altars, he continued to travel.[42] Hebron symbolizes the end of wandering, because it was there that Abraham changed his genealogy from a "wandering Jew" to a Jew with a homeland.

The pinnacle of his commentary is that the genealogy which Abraham passed to Isaac, and then on to Jacob, is still a part of Israel today. The trait of wandering, as Abraham did, is still a common stereotype for the "wandering Jews" of the Diaspora. Abraham altered his genes by falling in love with the ground beneath his feet. He remained in Hebron for 25 years and passed this attribute of love for the land to his son Isaac, as well as to countless Jews, like myself, who cannot bear to leave Israel even temporarily, unless for a very important reason. I always remember my mother's great-grandmother and her efforts for the Holy Land. It is her genealogy, as well as Abraham's, that gives me the feeling of a Jew whose eternal home is in Israel.

Hebron was a permanent settlement, and Abraham remained there for 25 years. Abraham raised his son, Isaac, in Hebron and it became Isaac's permanent home.

Isaac is the only forefather who spent his entire life in the Land of Israel. He was born in Israel and he

42. Genesis 12:9, 13:3.

died in Israel. While Isaac traveled a little throughout his life, he remained in the neighborhoods of Hebron, Beer Sheva, and the southern coast of the Mediterranean Sea. It was from Hebron that Jacob fled to Egypt, and also where Joseph left to look for his brothers.

Abraham purchased the cave where he buried Sarah, and as a result an eternal inheritance was awarded to him and passed on to Israel. Jacob's last request was to be buried with his kin, in the cave that Abraham purchased for a burial site.[43] This site became a magnet that has attracted generations of Jews to come and pray. Hebron was the location at which the Patriarchs and Matriarchs were laid to rest.

The Return and Two Tombs

Jacob spent over twenty years outside the land, in Aram (today's Syria). When he finally returned, he certainly had much to show for his efforts. Jacob was forced to run away in the shadow of his brother's threat to kill him. He came back home to the land with a large family of twelve sons, great wealth, and a reputation that drew Esau to seek him out and make peace with him.

Jacob crossed over the Jordan River into the Holy Land near Mahanaim, roughly east of Shechem. He then traveled through Shechem, Beth El,

43. Genesis 49:29-32.

Bethlehem, and Hebron. Benjamin, his youngest son, had the special merit of being the only son of Jacob to be born in the land. He came into the world as Jacob and his family were on their way to Hebron, but his birth ended tragically: *"So Rachel died and was buried on the way to Ephrath (that is, Bethlehem)."* [44]

Jacob erected a monument on Rachel's burial site. It was a monument that would cement the bonds Jacob wished to forge between the land and his descendants. *"And Jacob set a pillar on her grave, which is the pillar of Rachel's grave to this day."* [45] Sure enough, until this very day Rachel's Tomb can be seen just south of Jerusalem's municipal boundary.

Rachel's elder son, Joseph, was also buried in the Land of Israel. His bones were brought back to Shechem by the Israelites after the conquest of the land under Joshua. *"The bones of Joseph, which the children of Israel had brought up out of Egypt, they buried at Shechem, in the plot of ground which Jacob had bought from the sons of Hamor the father of Shechem for one hundred pieces of silver, and which had become an inheritance of the children of Joseph."* [46]

44. Genesis 35:19.
45. Genesis 35:20.
46. Joshua 24:32.

The Arab Sacrilege of Joseph's Tomb

I recently visited Joseph's Tomb, and came away bewildered and distraught to the depths of my soul. What had been a flourishing Jewish compound built to honor the memory of Joseph, is now completely burnt out and destroyed. Joseph's Tomb was a modern-yet-traditional holy site that had been preserved and developed over the course of three decades under Israeli control. A Torah study institution was established alongside it to ensure a loving Jewish presence. In October 2000, the tomb was burned almost to the ground in a matter of hours when it was taken over by Palestinian terrorists.

The inane Oslo Accords stipulated that the Tomb and the religious seminary adjoining it (named the "Joseph Still Lives" Yeshiva) would remain an Israeli oasis within the PA-controlled city of Shechem. This was a doomed arrangement from the start. The yeshiva students were barely able to bring in bare necessities. They were forced to travel into hostile territory and undergo meticulous searches at the hands of PA "policemen." Visitors and worshipers were restricted, and in general the Muslim goodwill necessary to make such an arrangement work was sadly lacking.

The present "Intifada" is often known more accurately as the Oslo War, in "honor" of the accords that enabled it. When radical Islamic leaders ignited the Intifada, Joseph's Tomb was unable to hold out for more than ten days. The fall began when an Israeli soldier was killed in one of the battles in Shechem. Mobs attacked the Israeli forces there, and started a fire at the holy site. Although then-Prime Minister Ehud Barak had said that we would not abandon any location in the face of Palestinian violence, the order was finally given: **Retreat!**

The retreating soldiers first removed all holy items, including Torah scrolls, prayer books, and Jewish texts, and only then surrendered the site to the PLO. Within minutes, the PLO terrorists began cruelly and viciously destroying any vestige of Jewish presence at the holy site. Even Arafat-apologist Shimon Peres said that the Arabs had thus shown that they "don't know how to preserve and respect holy sites."

Amidst all the words of condemnation and sorrow, Joseph's Tomb remained alone, desolate, and destroyed. It was heartbreaking to see Joseph abandoned and desecrated. For one Jew, it was much more than simply distressing.

Hillel Lieberman, a Rabbi born in the United States, was himself a part of the historic national homecoming of the Jewish people to the land. On the Sabbath only two days before Yom Kippur (Day of Atonement), the pinnacle of holiness in the Jewish calendar, young Rabbi Lieberman heard that Joseph's Tomb was in flames, and he instinctively set out to make his way there. He felt such a bond to Joseph that the inevitable dangers he faced as he entered the lion's den of bloodthirsty enemies were not even a consideration. The body of this holy man, violently murdered by Palestinians bent on destroying the Jewish connection to the land, was found the next day.

Shortly afterward his wife Yael said "If there is no Joseph's Tomb, then there is no Hillel! If he would have returned home [after hearing the news of the destruction], I would have been totally confused. I would have said, 'Excuse me, I don't understand; Joseph's Tomb is burning there, and you're here?' I wouldn't have believed it, I wouldn't have believed it...."

All that is now left of Joseph's Tomb is the deep pining of many thousands of Jews. The nearby Jewish communities of Elon Moreh, Itamar, Yitzhar, and Bracha expressed great sorrow as they longed for a glimpse of Joseph's Tomb, or for a chance to visit it again. Several hilltops in and around these communities still serve today as "observation points," for Jews to see Joseph's Tomb and pray for its redemption.

Currently, small groups of Jews are periodically allowed to visit the holy site with hardly any advance notice and usually in the middle of the night. I myself have participated in these visits. We try to remain hopeful and strong, but the sad sight of such devastation is hard to overcome.

As Jews, we cannot give in to despair. This is certainly not the first time we have faced tragedy and destruction. We are people of faith, believers, and sons of believers. In this case, we can only remain determined that we will yet return to Joseph's Tomb!

Our return to Joseph's Tomb can be achieved when we start taking the steps necessary to achieve peace. The first thing that we must do is to dismantle the Palestinian refugee camps established by the Arabs after the 1948 War of Independence. The threat to Joseph's Tomb comes from the nearby Balata refugee camp. This refugee camp, along with others, has been a source of terror and hatred for decades. The Muslims who murdered Jews trying to reach Joseph's Tomb and Jews traveling in its vicinity came from the Balata camp. A vast majority of Palestinian terrorists, who took the lives of over a thousand Israelis in countless suicide attacks initiated over the past four years, were residents of refugee camps as well. More than half a century after they were erected, it is about time these camps

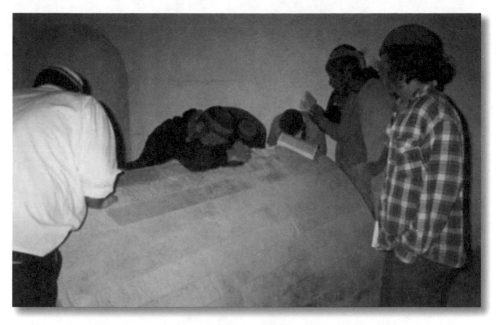

Jews visiting the burned tombs of Joseph, Menashe and Ephraim.

be dismantled and their residents moved to areas where they can be educated and rehabilitated in the larger Arab world.

The fact is that Arab intransigence has kept the 1948 refugees and their descendants clustered in miserable refugee camps, in order to artificially preserve the "Palestinian Problem." These camps indoctrinate generations of terrorists and suicide bombers. They serve as hotbeds of hatred and anti-Semitism, and perpetuate the poverty of their inhabitants. The refugee camps are inhumane, and the Palestinian people who have been forced to live in them have been robbed of any hope of freedom.

With the help of the free world, Israel can change this situation. My political plan includes the dismantling of all refugee camps from the West Bank and Gaza, including Balata. This will ensure Jewish territorial continuity from the communities of Elon Moreh and Bracha to the Tomb, and renew the Jewish presence in the town of Jacob and Joseph. Dismantling the camps and relocating the residents would also rectify a great atrocity against the Palestinian people.

The relocation of Palestinian refugees is not a new idea. In fact, a former President of the United States, Herbert Hoover, submitted a plan to relocate the Palestinian refugees in December of 1945. In 1949, when half a million refugees were created, he urgently wrote to the White House that "they [the Arab refugees] are in a deplorable condition" and their relocation "would give a permanent solution to the problem of these unfortunate people." [47]

---

47. Hoover & Truman: A Presidential Friendship. A Joint Project of the Truman & Hoover Presidential Libraries.
Letter from Herbert Hoover to the President of the United States.
http://trumanlibrary.org/hoover/internaltemplate.phptldate=1949-01-21&groupid=519 5&collectionid=hoover.

The Sad Solitude of Rachel's Tomb

Rachel's Tomb is a striking contrast to that of her son Joseph. Similarly a destination for worshipers seeking solace and inspiration, it stands proudly unbroken and seemingly timeless as a remembrance of Rachel's prayers and her descendants' bonds with this land:

"Thus says the Lord: A voice was heard in Ramah, Lamentation and bitter weeping, Rachel weeping for her children, Refusing to be comforted for her children, Because they are no more. Thus says the Lord: Refrain your voice from weeping, And your eyes from tears; For your work shall be rewarded, says the Lord, And they shall come back from the land of the enemy." [48]

Rachel's Tomb, in Bethlehem, is just a few hundred yards south of Jerusalem's municipal border. It enjoys several advantages over Joseph's Tomb. Due to its location so close to Jerusalem, it is accessible and remains in the national consciousness. Public buses frequently visit the site at regular hours, several times a day. It is also protected by a large concrete structure, so that the worshipers inside have nothing to fear. The area has been turned into a large synagogue and gathering hall, and families often gather there to mark festive occasions. However, these festivities are unfortunately celebrated in the shadows of great concrete walls and intensive security measures.

48. Jeremiah 31:14-15.

קבר רחל

Rachel's Tomb and the fortress which protects it.

Fortunately, the area around Rachel's Tomb is becoming increasingly Jewish. I have the great honor of working for the Jewish people with my friend and neighbor in Beth El, Chaim Silberstein, and with my friend and student from the neighboring community of Ofra, Yitzhak Mamo, in the field of reclaiming eastern Jerusalem neighborhoods and those nearby. We have succeeded in stirring the interest of many young couples who now live in these areas, and many Jews around the world who wish to take part in preserving Rachel's Tomb. They have agreed to take part in reclaiming and purchasing several buildings around the holy site. This success also comes thanks to the great deeds of people like Mrs. Evelyn Haies, president of Rachel's Children Reclamation Foundation in the U.S.

Chaim, Yitzhak, and other hard-working individuals envision an entire complex around Matriarch Rachel's burial place, which includes a study center, apartments, an events hall, and more. This is certainly a fitting, if partial, fulfillment of the prophecy, *"Stop your voice [Rachel] from weeping, and your eyes from tears, for your work will be rewarded, and your children will return from the land of the enemy."* [49]

49. Jeremiah 31:15.

The book of Genesis ends with Jacob's burial in the Machpelah Cave in Hebron. Jacob asked his children to "bring up my bones" to the Holy Land. In an impressive parade and ceremony, *"all the servants of Pharaoh, the elders of his house, and all the elders of the land of Egypt"* [50] accompanied Joseph's children into the land. Together they fulfilled his last wish. Genesis thus closes with the Fathers buried in the land, while the children were in their first Exile in Egypt, waiting to be reunited with their promised homeland.

50. Genesis 50:7-9.

CHAPTER THREE

WALKING
THE BIBLE'S PATH

Let us return to the story of our biblical forefathers; after all, here in the Holy Land, they are hard to stay away from. Let's discover the covenant of the land promised to Abraham, Isaac, and Jacob.

God's Covenant with Abraham

Our Patriarch Abraham traveled "the length and breadth" of the Land of Israel, just as God commanded him. ***"Now the Lord had said to Abram: Get out of your country, From your family And from your father's house, To a land that I will show you."*** [51] Abraham was suddenly uprooted from his home in Haran, destined to seek the land that God would show him.

Abraham arrived first in Shechem, then turned southward to Beth El, and continued towards the

Negev. He most likely traveled along or very near to today's Route 60. He thus set the course not only for thousands of modern travelers each day, but also for many of today's Jewish locations marking the history of his future descendants. From north to south, theses sites are:

- Joseph's Tomb.
- Eli, named after the High Priest who preceded Samuel.
- Shiloh, the site of the Tabernacle, Beth El, and Jerusalem.
- Rachel's Tomb in Bethlehem.
- The Cave of the Patriarchs in Hebron.

It is easy to fall into the routine of everyday life and rush past these sites. I am always refreshed and inspired when I look up and realize the singular, remarkable nature of the places that I pass every day.

The Legacy of Jacob

My neighbors and I identify most with Jacob, at least geographically. Jacob gave the name to our town: Beth El, Hebrew for "the House of God." Here he dreamt of the ladder ascending toward Heaven, with angels of the Lord climbing up and down its rungs. Beth El was the place where Jacob asked God to watch over him, and where he returned many years later to thank God for having fulfilled his request.

Beth El

Jacob's dream in Beth El represents an important lesson for us on several levels. For one thing, God confirmed the blessings Isaac had given to him: *"I am the Lord God of Abraham your father and the God of Isaac; the land on which you lie I will give to you and your descendants. Also your descendants shall be as the dust of the earth; you shall spread abroad to the west and the east, to the north and the south; and in you and in your seed all the families of the earth shall be blessed."* [52]

52. Genesis 28: 13-14.

Beth El Mayor Moshe Rosenbaum often likes to point out that on a clear day one can view, from Beth El, practically our entire small country: the snow-capped Mt. Hermon in the north, the coastal plain and the Mediterranean Sea to the west, Trans-Jordan to the east, and the hills of Hebron to the south. How reminiscent this scenery is of God's promise to Jacob, that his children would spread out to the four corners of the land.

Another fascinating feature of Jacob's dream is that it was truly a revelation for him: *"Then Jacob awoke from his sleep and said, Surely the Lord is in this place, and I did not know it. And he was afraid and said, How awesome is this place! This is none other than the house of God, and this is the gate of heaven!"* [53] Beth El thus represents the flash of realization that comes with a sudden renewal of faith.

How fitting it is that not only have we merited living in the "House of God," but we also have a Torah elementary school named "The Gate of Heaven." It is hard not to be inspired by our little angels studying the same Torah their forefathers received 3,000 years ago and thus climbing the rungs of the ladder towards Heaven.

53. Genesis 28:16-17.

Another aspect of Jacob's dream is found in a surprising place — in the rocks. Though today's Beth El has all the amenities of a modern city, Jacob didn't even have a pillow on which to rest his head. *"So he came to a certain place and stayed there all night, because the sun had set. And he took one of the stones of that place and put it at his head, and he lay down in that place to sleep."*[54] Our Sages teach that the stones argued among themselves for the right to be placed under the righteous man's head, until they all united into one rock so that all could share the privilege.

Let's now explore how God commanded Israel to settle the land that is His covenantal promise with Israel. As we have seen, prior to Joshua, the land was promised but not conquered and settled. The manifested reality of possessing the land begins in the days of Joshua.

54. Genesis 28:11.

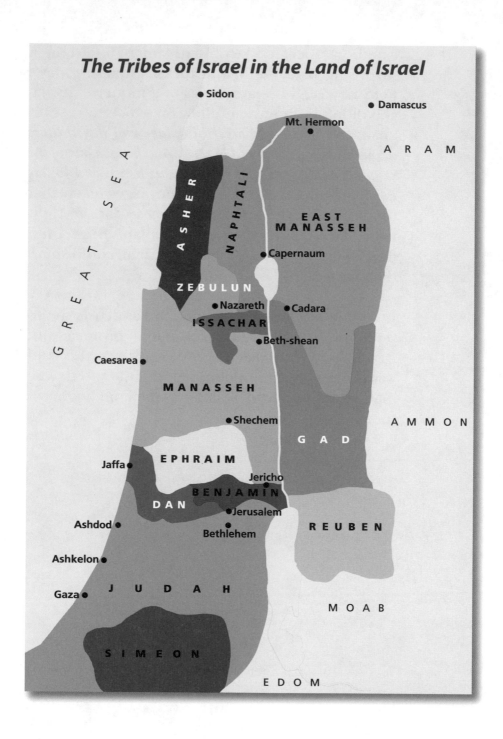

The Tribes of Israel in the Land of Israel

Taking Joshua's Route

We can gain abiding insights into God's plan for Israel by recalling God's direction to Joshua for possessing the land. God told Joshua:

"Moses, my servant, is dead. Now therefore, arise, go over this Jordan, you and all this people, to the land which I am giving to them-the children of Israel. Every place that the sole of your foot will tread upon I have given you, as I said to Moses. From the wilderness and this Lebanon as far as the great river, the River Euphrates, all the land of the Hittites, and to the Great Sea toward the going down of the sun, shall be your territory. No man shall be able to stand before you all the days of your life; as I was with Moses, so I will be with you. I will not leave you nor forsake you. Be strong and of good courage, for to this people you shall divide as an inheritance the land which I swore to their fathers to give them. Only be strong and very courageous, that you may observe to do according to all the law which Moses My servant commanded you; do not turn from it to the right hand or to the left, that you may prosper wherever you go." [55]

55. Joshua 1:2-7.

There is one continuous line connecting our past, present, and future. My wife Emuna, an author and columnist, wrote of this connection and her love of her homeland in an article for the "Jerusalem Report" magazine.

"Since September 1993 I have been among those who have seen the Oslo Accords as a stage in the wily Palestinian 'phased strategy' to eliminate Israel bit by bit. But my opposition to an Israeli withdrawal from Judea, Samaria and the Gaza District, doesn't just derive from my belief that such a retreat will endanger Israel within its pre-1967 boarders. Yes, I am convinced my presence here between Ramallah and Nablus makes an invaluable contribution to defending the Jewish state, and therefore to defending my family, but that is not what gives me the strength to drive the dangerous roads daily, by myself or with my children.

"Maybe it's not the accepted thing to say these days, but the real source of strength for me is the knowledge that a Jewish presence in Beth El, Shiloh and Hebron is natural and essential. Put differently: The main reason that I stay here is that this place is my historic homeland. The soil under the road from Beth El to Jerusalem is my soil. The hills looking down on that road are my hills. The trees and rocks behind which my would-be killers wait with their rifles are my trees and rocks. This place is mine, and I love it. I have no other place under the sun.

"I am not embarrassed to say this, even though many Israelis see attachment to the land as a reasonable value only when Arabs express it, whereas when expressed by Jews it becomes 'messianism' or 'paganism.' Love of one's motherland is imbibed with one's mother's milk among normal nations, but it seems that in the course of generations of being scattered in exile, the Jews have become a nation of luftmenchen, people of the air, who are still afraid of an earthly, simple love of their motherland. And it seems that the world, for its own reasons, has yet to recognize the right of the chosen people to emerge from the 'Old Testament' and live in the Holy Land in the same way that every nation lives in its own land." [56]

My home in Beth El is reminiscent of so many passages in the Book of Joshua. The children in the neighborhood sometimes play games such as "Conquer the Land," with "battles" taking place in our "neighboring kingdom" of Ai [57], or the cities of Jericho and Gibeon. [58]

The adults constantly remember the historic allocation of the land that Joshua, with divine guidance, made among the people of Israel. Beth El is a township within the geographical area known as the Binyamin Regional Council. No amount of gerrymandering can ever detach our biblical connections with the land as determined by Joshua the son of Nun.

56. Emuna Elon. "The Bottom Line: It's My Soil." The Jerusalem Report, August 2001 (p.55).
57. Joshua 8, 9.
58. Joshua 9:3.

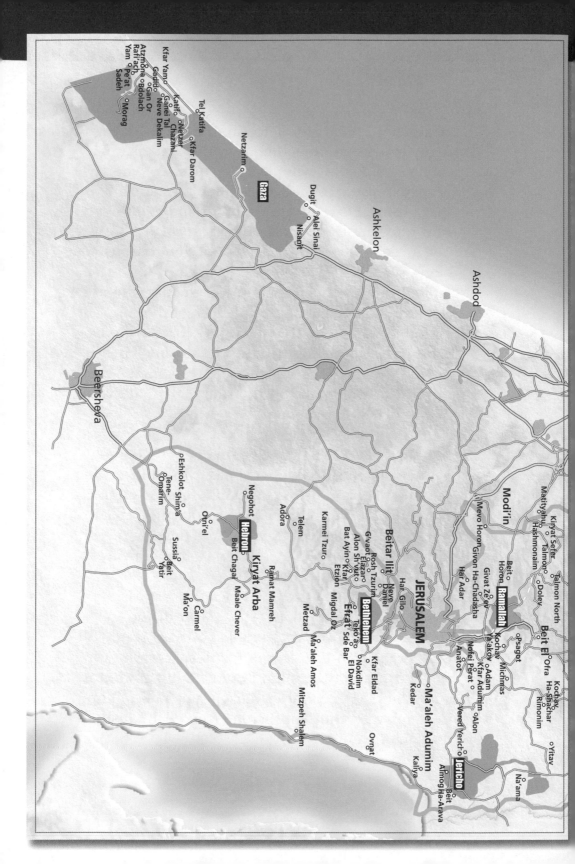

Picturing the Covenant with the Land

I travel to my home in Beth El from Jerusalem on the same route that Abraham and others traveled in Biblical times, from Shechem to Hebron and places in between. Today we pass many other beautiful and flourishing Jewish communities along the way, such as Adam, Psagot, Tel Tzion, and more. When I reach the Givat Assaf intersection, I am always inspired by the large sign posted there, sponsored by our local grocer.

"Here, in Beth El, 3,800 years ago, the Creator of the World promised the Land of Israel to the people of Israel. It is by virtue of this promise that we dwell today in Haifa, Tel Aviv, Shilo, and Hebron."

This sign has special significance for me. It speaks of God; it speaks of the people of Israel; and it speaks of the Bible and the course of history. History is the stage on which God acts and we see His will and way revealed.

This sign stands at the intersection known as Givat Assaf (Assaf Hill), named after Assaf Herskowitz. Assaf was a young husband and father from Ofrah, who was gunned down by Palestinian terrorists in May 2001. Tragically, only three months earlier, his own father, Aryeh Herskowitz, father of 5 and grandfather of 4, was similarly murdered in a Palestinian terrorist shooting attack only a few miles to the west.

Geulah Herskowitz, Assaf's mother and Aryeh's widow, still lives near Beth El in Ofrah. The suffering she was forced to go through is inconceivable, yet she showed the strength that has become the hallmark of residents of Judea and Samaria. The day after her son was murdered, she told visiting Prime Minister Ariel Sharon with disdain, "Foreign correspondents asked me yesterday if we had started thinking of leaving the country because of all the terrorism; they didn't ask me about leaving Judea and Samaria, but about leaving Israel altogether!" Clearly, leaving was the last thing on her mind.

Israeli history of the past several decades has proven that wherever the Arabs terrorize us, try to throw us out, and attempt to deny our God-given right to the land, there is where we thrive. A group of dedicated Jews, most of them young couples from nearby Beth El, moved to the hilltop at the Assaf intersection. They now provide a lookout position for soldiers to take up when necessary to deter would-be murderers from blocking our normal and happy lives. These fourteen families have made life much easier for us veteran residents. What once was a lonely turn-off onto the road towards Beth El is now a vibrant neighborhood manning the point. It has become a place to stand while waiting for rides, a spot to stop for a quick visit, and a reminder of God's faithfulness to Israel.

While on the topic of billboards, I am reminded of a large sign I once saw in the great city of Memphis, Tennessee. My late friend Ed McAteer took me to see one of 114 signs that he put up throughout the Bible Belt. Ed was a well-known preacher who helped Jerry Falwell found the Moral Majority. I will always fondly remember the day that we drove together to see the signs that he created to remind America of the covenant with Israel. Each sign contained a subtle message against the Bush Administration's Road Map plan that calls for an Arab Palestinian state right in the middle of the Holy Land.

Our leaders have unfortunately given into pressures to destroy this wonderful manifestation of the fulfillment of Jewish history. The weakness of the

'And the Lord said to Jacob... Unto thy offspring will I give this land.'

Pray that President Bush Honors God's Covenant with Israel. Call the White House with this message - (202) 456-1111."

current Israeli government has teamed up with an aggressive Western approach that refuses to recognize the biblical bonds tying us to this entire land. This is a threat to the entire glorious settlement enterprise of Judea, Samaria, and Gaza.[59]

The Current Political Situation in Israel

It is natural that Christian Zionists support the government of Israel and adopt the messages that come from Jerusalem. Christian Zionists recognize that the return of the people of Israel to their land is not a normal situation. Some Jews are still perplexed over this historic drama. Unfortunately, many Jews in Israel do not study the Bible, and have only a vague idea about their connection to their land, let alone the covenants.

59. For a detailed description of the land grant of the modern day Gaza Strip, see Joshua 15:20-47.

Many Israelis view the underlying cause of the ongoing struggle as our own policies, not those of our enemies. They regard the Jewish settlements in Judea, Samaria and Gaza as the reason for the violence in the Middle East. The quiet and God-loving communities, which maintained very good relationships with the local Arab communities before the rise of the PLO and the PA, are a ridiculous excuse for terror!

Israeli governments fall into this pit time after time. The Oslo Accords were signed as a peace treaty, and ended up as the catalyst for the wave of terror we have witnessed since October 2000, with a death toll of close to 1,300 victims, most of them civilians.

The Arabs call this war the al-Aqsa (the mosque on the Temple Mount) Intifada, pointing again to the heart of the conflict, the Temple Mount. The terrorists understand this, but current Israeli leaders do not. These leaders seem to ignore the basic facts of the conflict: the Jews have rights in this land and the Biblical covenant is true and significant.

The Oslo Accords developed into a bloody war and proved a tragic misinterpretation of the situation. The Israeli Prime Minister, Ariel Sharon, is making the same mistake all over again. His proposal to end this war is called "disengagement" but actually it has only one element: the uprooting of the Jewish presence in the Gaza Strip and Northern Samaria.

In these areas, Sharon has said, "there will be no Jews after 2005."

The prospect of forcing more than 8,000 Jews from their homes is horrific. The Jews of Gush Katif came to a barren and desolate land and have since been blessed with fertility and prosperity. The crops of Gush Katif yield fruit, vegetables, and flowers that sustain all of Israel. Crops grown in the Jewish fields of Gush Katif make up 60% of the produce exported from Israel.

Gush Katif is a block of Jewish settlements on the outskirts of the Gaza Strip. The distance between this block of homes and Gaza is greater than the distance from Gaza to Ashkelon. Gush Katif is further from Gaza than the private ranch of Prime Minister Ariel Sharon.

The Israeli Defense Forces disengaged from over 90% of the Gaza Strip more than 10 years ago, leaving these areas entirely under the rule of the Palestinian Authority. Israeli incursions into Gaza have occurred because thousands of kassam rockets have been launched from Palestinian controlled Gaza into Gush Katif and Sderot.

The term "disengagement" is clearly deceptive. Israel has already disengaged from the Arabs of Gaza. The only "disengagement" left is meant to deceive America and the world into uprooting Jews from their land. This would reward terrorism and send the message that it is only a matter of time until all the Jews, God forbid, are uprooted from the Land of Israel.

According to the disengagement plan, dozens of Jewish communities will be uprooted from Northern Samaria and the Gaza Strip in August of 2005. The terrorists will be rewarded with land that amounts to more than three times the land mass of the entire Gaza Strip. Cities in the north like Beth She'an, Afula, and Hadera will be in the range of kassam rockets just like Sderot in the South.

Those in favor of the withdrawal have said that Gaza never belonged to Israel and that Gaza holds no Biblical significance. Gaza is mentioned in the Bible more than 20 times. The land of Gaza was granted as an inheritance to the tribe of Judah.[60] Samson destroyed the pagan temple in Gaza.[61] The prophets Jeremiah, Amos, Zephaniah, and Zachariah all prophesied about Gaza.[62] Gaza was clearly part of the Biblical land grant to Israel and God has a plan for Gaza and its inhabitants in the future. As the preparations for this withdrawal increase, please keep the inhabitants of Gaza and northern Samaria in your hearts and prayers. The People of the Book have a responsibility to uphold and protect the covenant between God and Israel.

Our dedication to the biblical cause cannot rely on the Israeli government, or on any government. The government of Israel has decided against the

---

60. Joshua 15:21-47
61 Judges 16:1-31
62. Jeremiah 47:1; Amos 1:6; Zephaniah 2:4; Zechariah 9:5

covenant and against any national interest, by accepting Sharon's disengagement plan. As a cabinet minister (responsible for the tourism portfolio) I tried to stop Sharon from this dangerous decision. Unfortunately, I have not yet succeeded and I have found myself outside the cabinet.

I remain a member of the Knesset (Israel's parliament) and try my best to stop the dangerous policy of uprooting Jews from Israel, and to prevent disengagement from our biblical roots, from our covenant, and from our land.

I continue to remind the citizens of Israel of our God-given right and of our responsibility to this land. This is not an easy road to travel, and I have found myself isolated from those of my colleagues who are willing to forfeit the covenant in order to appease terrorists.

We must win this battle. After Gaza and Northern Samaria will come the battles for Shechem, Beit El, Bethlehem, Hebron, and Jerusalem. All these areas will be sacrificed to compensate the terrorists' appetite. We must remember that the battle for Israel is not for the Gaza Strip and the West Bank. The Palestinian education system teaches that all of Israel belongs to the Arabs. When they succeed in pushing the Jews into the sea, heaven forbid, the Palestinians will own all of Israel, from the Jordan River to the Mediterranean Sea.

The creation of a Palestinian state in the Gaza Strip and Northern Samaria would create an Islamic-Jihad terror state that would risk the very existence of Israel as well as the free world. If we do not stop the disengagement plan now, we will watch helplessly as the plan to take Israel inch by inch is realized. We need your help, and we have faith that it will be forthcoming.

The following chapter is my proposed plan for peace in Israel. "The Right Road to Peace Plan" considers the Palestinian situation and provides solutions for the Palestinian people. "The Right Road to Peace Plan" will provide opportunities that they have never had before. They will have the opportunity to provide for their families and to taste freedom. This plan provides for Israeli security and guards the Biblical covenant with the children of Israel for this land.

CHAPTER FOUR

THE RIGHT ROAD
TO PEACE

"You shall dispossess the inhabitants of the land and dwell in it, for I have given you the land to possess." [63]

The biblical principle that "The Land of Israel belongs to the people of Israel" formed the foundation for the Return to Zion. Unfortunately, to many this foundation seems to be irrelevant when dealing with the Israeli-Arab conflict. The various peace plans that have been proposed for decades have taken a heavy toll of lives from the Israelis. Each plan has been based on an attempt to ignore the fundamental principle that God gave this land to Israel. Consequently they have all failed.

This blatant disregard of God's covenant is a case of burying one's head in the sand.

The Jewish people's return to their land is the major geo-political factor in the Middle East. This is in fact a miraculous event: A nation that was absent from its land for hundreds of years is now returning to it, by being uprooted from the countries in which it has been dispersed. Only those who read the Bible can understand this phenomenon and are capable of proposing a realistic political solution. Peace will only be achieved after acceptance of the Return to Zion, acceptance that must begin in Israeli society and spread to all the nations involved.

Those who desire peace in Israel must examine ways to achieve real and lasting peace. They must identify the roots of the conflict that is spilling our blood, and must seek a solution with honesty and creativity. Those who make an effort to study the questions at hand and the forces acting in this region, discover that the sole chance to achieve peace lies with a plan based on Israeli sovereignty extending over the entire width of Israel, from the Jordan to the Mediterranean. This is the plan presented here.

The Israeli-Arab conflict focuses on two points.

- The first issue is that of the land: To whom does this land belong? Does the Land of Israel belong to the Jewish people, or is it merely another Arab estate?

- The second issue is the question of the Arab refugees: What should be done with the refugees who fled from the bounds of Israel during the 1948 War of Independence, and have retained their status as refugees until the present?

These two questions may be answered in only one of two ways:

The first way is that the land is an Arab one. This approach also implies the answer to the question of the refugees, in the form of the "Right of Arab refugees to return to their former homes." Such an answer turns the entire Zionist movement into an illegitimate colonial one, and leads directly to the destruction of Israel as a Jewish State, and to the reversal of the process of the ingathering of the exiles.

The second answer is based on the recognition and the certainty that the Bible is true, and therefore the Land of Israel belongs to the Jewish people. This belief should motivate us to strive to achieve the rapid and generous rehabilitation of Arab refugees in Arab countries. This is the sole solution. Any partition of the land and any delay in the rehabilitation of the refugees means the adoption of the PLO strategy of perpetuating the conflict, a strategy aimed at implementing the first approach: the destruction of the State of Israel.

Only those who know and believe the Biblical verses: *"To you and to your seed I shall give this land, forever,"* [64] and *"Do not fear them,"* [65] are capable of leading the State of Israel to stand up for its own interests, and advance a peace plan based on Israeli sovereignty and on solving the problem of the Arab refugees created in the War of Independence.

While the Biblical covenant serves as our inspiration, those who possess belief must propose a real alternative. A political plan that addresses all issues involved in the conflict in the Middle East, and that is based on accepted principles of international law, is essential in order to advance the vision of the Return to Zion in the world of political action. This plan is one of two or three major alternative peace plans considered today by the Israeli public for future implementation. It is presented to you on the following pages.

64. Genesis 13:15.
65. Deuteronomy 20:3.

"The Palestinian Problem," has been fueling the Israeli-Arab conflict for two generations. It is used to strengthen the Arab claim in the debate over whom this land belongs to.

It is not by chance that the "Right of Return" and the rehabilitation of the refugees were kept as open issues in all of the accords signed with the Palestinians: It is part of the strategic plan to avoid a resolution of the conflict.

All plans that are based on the partition of Western Israel into two entities, "Palestine" and Israel, are disastrous from the security and Biblical point of view. Such programs offer no solution to the Palestinian problem, because they propose to the Palestinians no more than a tiny and densely populated quasi-state, totally dependant on the Israeli economy.

Additionally, an integral assumption of these plans is that the land does not belong to the people of Israel. These two characteristics ensure a strengthening of the Arab war towards the destruction of Israel as the Jewish state.

From every aspect — geographic, economic, and demographic — it is clear that it will be impossible to resolve the problem within the small, overcrowded area between the Jordan River and the Mediterranean Sea.

Only with application of a **regional solution,** that includes the entire territory of British Mandatory Palestine (Land of Israel), can the peace process be delivered from its impasse. Only a regional solution, based on **geopolitical and economic logic,** can provide the Middle East with long-term peace, prosperity, and stability.

The American and British victory in Iraq has spurred an American commitment to instill **democratic values** in the Middle East and establish a new political map. This is an historic opportunity to enable the Arab nations to be part of the solution to the Palestinian problem and garner **international support and funding**.

The Right Road to Peace Plan addresses the fundamental issues related to the conflict and offers a comprehensive solution for Israel, Palestinian Arabs, and surrounding countries. Expanding the solution to include both sides of the Jordan River creates a new reality in which:

- Israelis and Palestinian Arabs exist alongside one another in two genuine, sovereign states, seeking stability and peace.

- A well-defined natural border would be established, far from population centers.

- Both states would have strategic depth and ample land reserves.

Dealing directly with final status issues, the Right Road to Peace Plan offers:

- Removal of the threat to Israel's existence as a Jewish state.

- Realization of the covenant regarding the ownership of the Land of Israel.

- The granting of national expression and full rights for all Palestinian Arabs.

- Building an opportunity to remove the demographic threat of Israeli Arabs.

- Full and comprehensive rehabilitation of Palestinian refugees.

- An immediate permanent-status settlement to end the conflict.

Key Principles of the
Right Road to Peace Plan

Dissolution of the Palestinian Authority

1. Immediate dissolution of the Palestinian Authority, a non-viable entity with no future,
   whose existence precludes the termination of
   the conflict.

Eradication of terror infrastructure

2. Israel will uproot the Palestinian terror infrastructure. All arms will be collected, incitement
   will be stopped, and all the refugee camps,
   which serve as incubators for terror, will be dismantled. Terrorists and their direct supporters
   will be deported.

Recognition and Development of Jordan
as the Palestinian State

3. Israel, the United States, and the international
   community will recognize the Kingdom of Jordan as the only legitimate representative of the
   Palestinians. Jordan will once again recognize
   itself as the Palestinian nation-state.

   In the context of a regional economic development program, Israel, the United States, and
   the international community will put forth a
   concerted effort for the long-term development of Jordan, to rehabilitate its economy and
   enable it to absorb a limited number of refugees within its borders.

Israeli sovereignty over Judea, Samaria and Gaza

4. Israeli sovereignty will be asserted over Judea, Samaria (the West Bank), and Gaza.

   The Arab residents of these areas will become citizens of the Palestinian state in Jordan.

   The status of these citizens, their connection to the two states, and the manner of administration of their communal lives will be decided in an agreement between the governments of Israel and Jordan (Palestine).

   Palestinian-Jordanian citizenship will be offered subsequently to the Arab citizens of Israel.

Rehabilitation of refugees and completion of population exchange

5. Israel, the United States, and the international community will allocate resources for the completion of the exchange of populations that began in 1948, as well as the full rehabilitation of the refugees and their absorption and naturalization in various countries.

Peace and Normalization

6. After implementation of the above stages, Israel and Jordan- Palestine will declare the conflict terminated. Both sides will work to normalize peaceful relations between all parties in the region.

Clarification of Key Principles
The Dissolution of the Palestinian Authority and the War on Terror:

1. Immediate dissolution of the Palestinian Authority, a non-viable entity with no future whose existence precludes the termination of the conflict.

2. Israel will uproot the Palestinian terror infrastructure. All arms will be collected, incitement will be stopped, and all the refugee camps, which serve as incubators for terror, will be dismantled. Terrorists and their direct collaborators will be deported.

The Palestinian Authority — An obstacle to peace. After the eradication of the Taliban and the regime of Saddam Hussein, it follows logically that another of the world's most dangerous regimes, the Palestinian Authority (PA), be dissolved:

- **The PA has funded and dispatched homicide terrorists to carry out terror attacks in Israel.**

- Senior PA officials have plundered large sums from funds contributed by donor nations.

- The PA is indoctrinating its children toward hatred and violence.

- The PA plays a leading role in the international terror network.

- PA strategy is to pay lip service in the western media to "peace," while delivering the opposite message for domestic consumption.

The absence of responsible leadership in Judea, Samaria, and Gaza encourages criminal activity, Islamic extremism and long-term damage to the infrastructure and ecology of the region. Israeli control over Judea, Samaria and Gaza will be a stabilizing influence.

The establishment of a Palestinian state in Judea, Samaria and Gaza would:

- Foster, continue, and intensify terror.

- Perpetuate day-to-day friction between Jews and Arabs.

- Represent a constant demographic danger to the very existence of Israel as a Jewish state.

Such a state, dissected, demilitarized, its economy totally dependent on Israel, would evolve into a protectorate whose main function would be to supply cheap labor to the State of Israel.

It would be unable to provide its citizens with national pride, civic freedoms, or economic hope, and offers no solution to the refugee problem.

The cessation of terror — using military means:
The Camp David talks between Ehud Barak and Yasser Arafat in the summer of 2000 brought in their wake an unprecedented wave of terror. With the encouragement and funding of the Palestinian Authority, many hundreds of Israelis have been killed and thousands injured in terror attacks. Proportionately, Israel has sustained losses equivalent to ten times the number of Americans killed in the 9/11 tragedy.

Israel's generous territorial offers and support of the Palestinian Authority did not stop the terror. Furthermore, equipping it with arms has caused terror to mushroom to intolerable proportions.

Israel's intense and relentless military activity against the terrorist strongholds in the Palestinian Authority led to a dramatic drop in the number of attacks.

Today more than ever, the world understands that the only way to fight terror is by firm and unequivocal action. Israel has the means to dismantle the Palestinian Authority and its security apparatus quickly and efficiently.

Refugee camps — hotbeds of terror:
The refugee camps lying alongside the Arab cities in Judea, Samaria, and Gaza must be dismantled. Dominated by poverty, despair, and virulent hatred, the refugee camps breed terror. They produce the

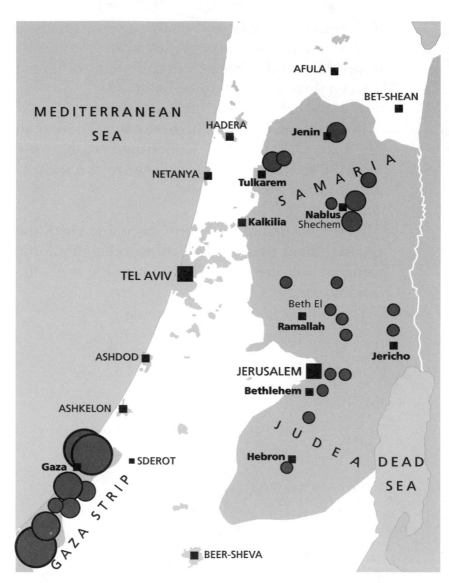

MEDITERRANEAN
SEA

AFULA

BET-SHEAN

HADERA

Jenin

S A M A R I A

NETANYA

Tulkarem

Kalkilia

Nablus
Shechem

TEL AVIV

Beth El

Ramallah

Jericho

ASHDOD

JERUSALEM

Bethlehem

ASHKELON

J U D E A   DEAD

SEA

Gaza

SDEROT

Hebron

G A Z A   S T R I P

BEER-SHEVA

Refugee camps in Judea, Samaria and Gaza. It was here that most of the bomb factories and weapon caches were discovered and from here that most of the terrorists originate.

motivation for terror and enable terror squads to be formed, providing them with a safe haven. The population of the camps is at the mercy of terrorists and provides cover for their activities.

The continued existence of these camps more than fifty years after they were established is a humanitarian disgrace, as well as a threat to the security and peace of the Middle East.

The dismantling of the camps, combined with the establishment of a mechanism to rehabilitate the refugees, will strike a mortal blow to the terror infrastructure.

Recognition and Development of Jordan as the Palestinian State

3. Israel, the United States, and the international community will recognize the Kingdom of Jordan as the only legitimate representative of the Palestinians. Jordan will once again recognize itself as the Palestinian nation-state. In the context of a regional economic development program, Israel, the United States, and the international community will put forth a concerted effort for the long-term development of Jordan, to rehabilitate its economy and enable it to absorb a limited number of Palestinian refugees within its borders.

The Hashemite kingdom of Jordan is in fact a Palestinian state:

Both sides of the Jordan River are considered "Land of Israel" in the Bible. The Jews have never conceded their claim to the land of Reuben, Gad and Menasheh on the eastern side of the river. Nevertheless, Israeli Jews recognize the fact that there has been an Arab Palestinian state on these lands since 1922 — the Hashemite Kingdom of Jordan.

At the end of WWI, the League of Nations convened in San Remo and gave Britain a mandate over Palestine — east and west together — so it would build there a "National Home for the Jewish people." In contradiction to this mandate, in 1922 Britain gave all the eastern part of this territory to Abdallah, the Hashemite prince, and established an Arab-Palestinian state there, decades before the Jewish state was established.

In 1948, Jordan crossed the Jordan River to the west, and took control over what was known from then on as "the West Bank" — Judea and Samaria, the mountainous heartland of Western Palestine and the ancient Jewish kingdoms. Jordan unilaterally annexed these areas and granted citizenship to all its Arab population, both residents and refugees. It enacted a number of major constitutional amendments expressing Palestinian- Jordanian unity.

For many years, the PLO competed with Jordan over who represents the Palestinian Arabs. Only after Israel's weak response to the first "intifada" in 1987, and the subsequent strengthening of the PLO, which resulted in Israel viewing the PLO as the representative of the Palestinian Arabs, did Jordan withdraw from its connection with the "West Bank."

The new reality in the Middle East provides an historic opportunity to rectify that error and once again establish Jordan as the Palestinian nation-state — the exclusive representative of the Palestinian Arabs.

From Refugees to Citizens Once Again:
On July 31, 1988 Jordan revoked the Jordanian citizenship of all the Arabs living in Judea, Samaria, and Gaza. As a Palestinian state, Jordan-Palestine will return this citizenship. Even if they choose to continue to live in Israel, these citizens will enjoy national and political rights in the Palestinian state, whose capital is Amman.

NOTE: *In February 2003 twenty-two Palestinian unions in Judea, Samaria and Gaza appealed secretly to King Abdallah for his economic intervention in these areas — despite their knowledge of Arafat's strong objection to such machinations. This act testifies to the fact that the current mood would support the renewed link with Jordan and the dissolution of the Palestinian Authority.*

No to a Second Palestinian state:
A Palestinian state in Judea, Samaria, and Gaza would in fact mean the establishment of a second Palestinian state. This would not be a solution of "two states for two nations," but rather "three states for two nations" — one for the Jews and two for the Palestinians.

A second Palestinian state in Judea, Samaria, and Gaza would pose a threat to both Israel and Jordan. It would serve as a springboard to turn all of the Land of Israel — from the Iraqi desert to the Mediterranean Sea — into a single Palestinian Arab state.

What would Jordan gain from becoming part of the regional settlement?

The current Jordanian regime is friendly to Israel and for the most part its stability, however, is currently in danger because of its delicate pro-Western geopolitical status.

The lack of clarity concerning the status of its Palestinian majority and the danger posed to it by the establishment of an additional Palestinian state would foment unrest among the Palestinian population of Jordan against the government.

The dissolution of the Palestinian Authority and the subjugation of the PLO establishment would elicit a sigh of relief in Amman and pave the way for the underscoring of the Palestinian character of Jordan, whose absolute majority — including the Queen and numerous senior government officials — is Palestinian.

A comprehensive development program for Jordan, accompanied by moderate reforms to bolster its Palestinian character, is likely to be welcomed in Amman and would move the kingdom forward to a more hopeful future.

Jordan's principal problems are economic. It could be significantly strengthened by Israel and the United States in the context of a regional "Marshall Plan" integrated with the rebuilding of Iraq.

A comprehensive, internationally funded development plan for Jordan, most of whose territory is undeveloped, would facilitate the absorption and naturalization of the Arabs of Judea, Samaria, and Gaza.

Israel has a profound interest in the development of Jordan as a Palestinian state. The transfer to Jordan of significant portions of American military aid to the Middle East could significantly transform Jordan's economy. The normalization of relations and cessation of hostilities would significantly reduce the need for major U. S. foreign defense aid, part of which could also be reallocated to boost Jordan's economy.

Palestinian Flag   **Jordan's Flag**

Jordan is Palestine!

KEEPING THE PERSPECTIVE — SEEING THE WHOLE PICTURE

Do we, the only Jewish state, not have a right to secure and recognized borders?

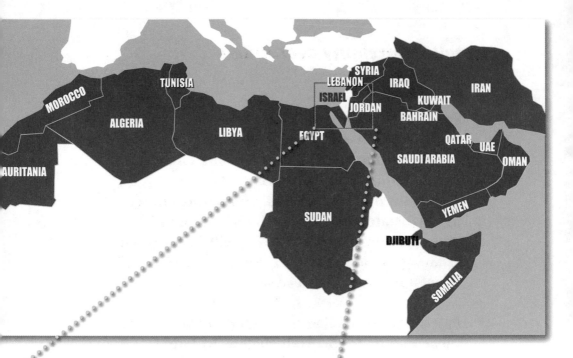

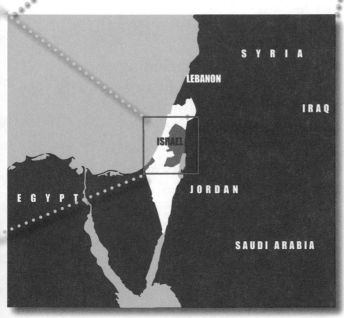

The Arab territories are spread over from the Atlantic Ocean to the Persian Gulf.
Within this vast space, 500 times the size of Israel, is the Jewish state who claims its right for sovereignty in the tiny area that it inhabits.

Should this small and densely populated area be the only solution to a troubled region?

Has it not been proven time after time that this constrained solution is impossible?

☐ *Israel (including Judea, Samaria and Gaza) — 10,800 sq miles (28,000 sq km)*
■ *The 20 states of the Arab League — 5,500,000 sq miles (14,240,650 sq km)*
■ *Iran (not member of the Arab League) — 636,370 sq miles (1,648,200 sq km)*

Israeli Sovereignty over Judea, Samaria, and Gaza

4. Israeli sovereignty will be asserted over Judea, Samaria (the West Bank), and Gaza. The Arab residents of these areas will become citizens of the Palestinian state in Jordan.
    The status of these citizens, their connection to the two states, and the manner of administration of their communal lives, will be decided in an agreement between the governments of Israel and Jordan (Palestine).

    Palestinian-Jordanian citizenship will be offered subsequently to the Arab citizens of Israel.

Assertion of sovereignty — Restoration of stability.

The areas of Judea, Samaria, and Gaza, including the eastern part of Jerusalem, were part of the British mandate territory that was intended for the establishment of the Jewish homeland. Since the end of the British mandate, these areas did not receive any recognized legal status. They were annexed by Jordan after the War of Independence, but were never recognized as part of Jordan in international law.

During the Six Day War in 1967, Israel liberated these territories and returned them to the Jewish people. Eastern Jerusalem was officially annexed to the State of Israel in 1981.

The status of the remainder of these areas remained unclear. Israel evaded determining the future of these areas. This encouraged Palestinian aspirations for establishing an additional Palestinian state in these areas, which, through their topographical advantage, directly threaten the densely populated Israeli coastal plain and Jerusalem basin.

The areas of Judea, Samaria, and Gaza are among the only places in the western world where Jews cannot move without fear, where extensive Arab criminal activity is openly carried out, and where there is wide spread abuse of environmental issues. Assertion of Israeli sovereignty on these areas will end this grave situation.

As part of the plan to end the conflict and create a new and stable map in the Middle East, **the border between Palestine and Israel must be drawn at the Jordan River**, and all the areas west of the Jordan must be formally annexed to the State of Israel.

Judea and Samaria — The Cradle of Jewish Civilization

Judea and Samaria represent the historical "spinal cord" of the Land of Israel. The central mountain range, whose heart is Jerusalem, reminds us of who we are. It was here that Abraham walked with his son, Isaac and here Jacob set up his tents. It was here that our forefathers, under Joshua, conquered this land by divine decree from the Canaanite nations.

In the hills of Judea and Samaria we find dozens of holy sites and a myriad of others with historic importance, many of which have not yet been researched. The handing over of Beit El, Shiloh, Bethlehem, and Hebron to foreign (hostile) hands would signify the severance of the Jewish people from its roots and lead ultimately to the loss of recognition of their right to the land.

The Biblical and eternal capital of Israel, Jerusalem, is surrounded on three sides by Judea and Samaria. **Whoever is concerned for the future of Jerusalem — and is aware of its centrality in the prophetic vision of the return to Zion — cannot allow it to become once again a border settlement in the heart of hostile Arab land.**

In the hills of Judea and Samaria and the Gaza coastal plain we have witnessed the development of Jewish villages and towns that manifest national strength and exceptional individual and communal quality. Unsettling these places would be a devastating moral blow to Israel that is liable to damage the very fabric of society and create a severe civil crisis.

The status of the Palestinian Arabs

In the framework of the eradication of terror, the terrorist heads and inciters will be deported from Judea, Samaria, and Gaza. The dismantling of the refugee camps, part of the rehabilitation process, will reduce the Arab population in these areas and lessen the poverty and density in the Palestinian Arab towns.

The Arab population that will continue to reside within the new areas of the State of Israel, will benefit from the civil rights conferred by Israel, but its citizenship will be Palestinian, and its political rights will be actualized in Amman.

The actual administration governing the Arab sector will derive its authority from the Israeli sovereign, but will enjoy limited autonomy in a form to be determined in negotiations between Israel and the Hashemite Kingdom of Palestine.

This distinction between residency and citizenship is also valuable for the Arabs living in Israel today. Those residents who would prefer not to declare loyalty to the Jewish state could realize their political rights in Amman's parliament. In this way, the Jewish character of the state of Israel will be strengthened without uprooting anyone.

In order to keep its Jewish character in the future, the Israeli government will adopt a systematic policy of encouraging emigration of Arabs from all of the Land of Israel, and will help anyone who wishes to find their future in other countries.

Dialogue Between States — A Positive Dynamic.
The negotiations with the Hashemite Kingdom regarding the precise status of the residents of Judea, Samaria, and Gaza will differ in its essence from those conducted until today between Israel and the Palestinian Authority. **When the two parties to discussions are sovereign nations, both of whom are interested in stability and peace, it is possible to reach a real solution.**

It is even possible to postpone some of the harder decisions for the future, with the confidence that a positive dynamic of cooperation and mutual interests will develop over the years. As is well known, agreements between democratic nations last for many years. Israel is a true democracy, while the Hashemite Kingdom is a constitutional monarchy undergoing a process of democratization. It has one of the most progressive regimes in the Arab world, with a clearly pro-Western orientation.

The Rehabilitation of the Refugees and Completion of Population Exchange:

5. **Israel, the United States and the international community will allocate resources for the completion of the exchange of populations that began in 1948 and the full rehabilitation of the refugees and their absorption and naturalization in various countries.**

6. **After implementation of the above stages, Israel and Jordan-Palestine will declare the conflict terminated. Both sides will work to normalize peaceful relations between all parties in the region.**

The Refugee Problem Must be Resolved

The refugee problem in the Middle East has burgeoned into dangerous proportions, in sharp contrast with all other refugee populations from the 1940s, who were resettled and rehabilitated decades ago.

From a few hundred thousand Arab refugees in 1948, Palestinian refugees now number in the millions, including second and third generations. Their refugee status is not only the product of education and propaganda, but also the result of many years of neglect and lack of desire on the part of the Arab world to rehabilitate them.

The resolution of the refugee problem must be a primary element of any final status arrangement. For many years the Arab world has done its best not to rehabilitate the refugees in order to undermine Israel's right to exist.

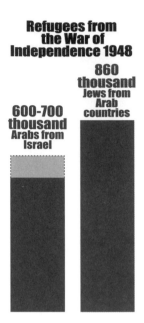

Refugees from the War of Independence 1948

860 thousand Jews from Arab countries

600-700 thousand Arabs from Israel

An important ingredient in the resolution of the refugee issue is predicated on international insistence on the need to rehabilitate the refugees and the reallocation of American foreign defense aid to the absorption of refugees.

It's Time to Complete the Population Exchange Begun in 1948

The relocation and rehabilitation of the Palestinian refugees in Arab lands will complete the population exchange process begun in 1940.

- **The State of Israel absorbed millions of Jewish refugees from all over the world and, within a few years, these refugees became citizens of the state with full rights.**

- Almost one million of these refugees fled from Arab lands leaving behind property and wealth for which they were never compensated.

At the same time, the 1948 War of Independence created hundreds of thousands of Arab refugees who fled to Arab lands.

While the Jews displaced from Arab lands were rehabilitated and naturalized in Israel, the Arab countries refused to do the same for Arab refugees.

The resettlement of these refugees and their descendants will complete a historic circle of population exchange. This will result in the emergence of countries where the majority of their population shares a common nationality and culture.

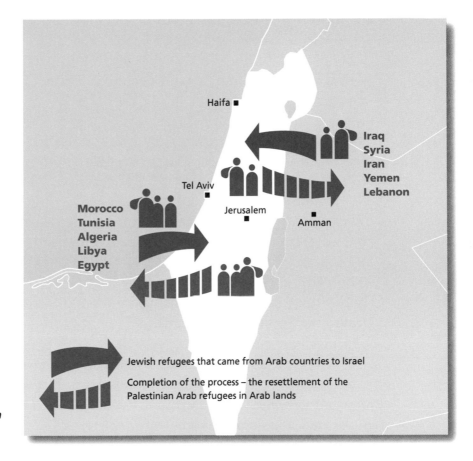

The closing of the historic circle of population exchange in the Middle East and the rehabilitation of the refugees.

Haifa ■

Iraq
Syria
Iran
Yemen
Lebanon

Tel Aviv ■

Morocco
Tunisia
Algeria
Libya
Egypt

Jerusalem ■

Amman ■

Jewish refugees that came from Arab countries to Israel

Completion of the process – the resettlement of the Palestinian Arab refugees in Arab lands

The End of the Process

Various peace processes initiated between Israel and the Palestinian Arabs until now have all failed to bring about the end of the conflict. The principle reason for this is that the PLO, the Palestinian Authority, and its leaders remain intransigent and have no interest in terminating the conflict. This is indicative of the fact that the PA is not a genuine peace partner and in fact is a hindrance to peace.

In contrast, however, the Right Road to Peace can bring about the end of the conflict, because:

- The parties of the final-status settlement are sovereign states that have a vested interest in peace and stability.

- The basic issues will be unequivocally dealt with, leaving no prospect for the future destruction of the State of Israel.

- Weapons will be confiscated, weapons factories destroyed, and the refugee camps dismantled.

- The refugee issue will be resolved as all refugees will be granted citizenship and the potential for economic rehabilitation.

*The Right Road to Peace proposes a **simple**, sustainable solution that achieves **historic justice** and advances the **vision of the prophets.** It addresses the **human tragedies** of all the sides and does not harm Israeli **deterrence.***

Underlying Principles of the Right Road to Peace:

No other proposal addresses final-status issues. The Right Road to Peace offers a way to translate the achievements of the war in Iraq into a new "Marshall Plan" for the Middle East, a plan that is based on Israel, the only stable democracy in the region, and on Jordan which has a quasi-democratic government, thus removing the Palestinian terrorist regime from the picture. This plan is a our way to take part in the realization of the prophecy and the Covenant, between the Lord and His people, and between His people and His land.

The Right Road to Peace manifests:

Biblical Validity

God gave this land (Canaan, later called Palestine) to the people of Israel — the descendants of Abraham, Isaac, and Jacob. The historical continuity of God's people, Israel, with God's covenant has been unbroken since patriarchal times and was reaffirmed in the Torah and Neviim (prophetic books of history) commonly called in the Christian world "the Old Testament" (Covenant).

People of the Book (Jews and Christians) who recognize the ultimate authority of God's Word for all of history understand that what God declared stands as covenant truth through the ages and cannot be altered by human will or force. This plan is the only practical plan based on the Bible.

Simplicity

Two states for two nations on either side of the Jordan River. This solution offers a natural and logical border, separation of hostile populations and an end to the human tragedy that has continued since the War of Independence.

Sustainability

This plan grants the Palestinian Arabs citizenship in a real state that has the ability to sustain itself economically and politically, with clearly defined borders. This state would not find itself in constant conflict with Israel and its future would not be predicated on the destruction of Israel as a Jewish state.

Morality

This plan prioritizes the treatment of human issues over empty symbols. "Peace" proposals that are based on continued conflict perpetuate poverty, violence and ignorance. The Right Road to Peace brings about a solution to the Palestinians' suffering without capitulating to terror and violence.

Deterrence

An Israeli withdrawal of any kind would severely harm Israel's national strength while reinforcing the motivation for terror. The Right Road to Peace preserves Israel's deterrent capabilities, making it possible for the first time to delineate secure and recognized borders.

Justice

The secure existence of Israel corrects an historic injustice. The essence of Zionism is to establish a state for the Jewish people, a safe haven for millions of Jewish refugees from all over the world including from the Arab countries.

The Arab world must be involved in a resolution of the Arab refugee issue, using its vast territorial expanses and abundant natural resources.

This is not only justice in its most elementary sense — that of human decency — but also draws on deep Biblical sources, which view the Jewish people as a nation with a unique destiny and place in history.

This plan is founded on the fundamental historic and Biblical truth that the Land of Israel belongs to the Jewish people.

However, it realizes only part of this principle because it accepts the existence of a Palestinian state east of the Jordan River, part of the Biblical Land of Israel.

The realization of the Zionist dream — the return of the Jewish people to its land from all corners of the earth — is a historic event of global significance.

Only when Israel's Arab neighbors accept its right to exist within secure boundaries as a fundamental reality will regional peace and prosperity be achieved.

The Wrong Road

Idea: Palestinian state between the Jordan River and the Mediterranean.

Result: A tiny, overcrowded, dissected and demilitarized Israeli protectorate alongside a threatened Jewish state devoid of strategic depth.

The areas of the "Palestinian state" (in red) according to the Sharon proposal. This area is designated for over 2.5 million (!) Palestinian Arabs prior to the absorption of those dispersed in Arab lands.

Israel	Palestinian Authority
Per Capita Domestic Product	Per Capita Domestic Product
$19,000	**$1,540**

The initial figures for the Palestinian economy in Judea, Samaria and Gaza guarantee continued economic dependence on the modern and developed Israeli economy.

Two State Solution

The Right Road

Idea: Israeli sovereignty between the Jordan River and
the Mediterranean.
Result: A viable Palestinian State east of the Jordan River
– unfragmented, having natural borders and no friction.

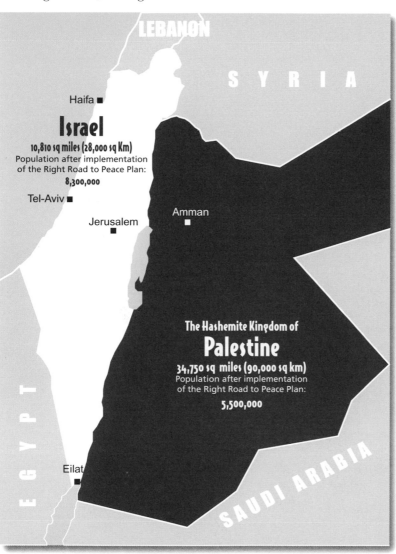

LEBANON

SYRIA

Haifa ■

Israel
10,810 sq miles (28,000 sq Km)
Population after implementation
of the Right Road to Peace Plan:
8,300,000

Tel-Aviv ■

Amman
■

Jerusalem
■

The Hashemite Kingdom of
Palestine
34,750 sq miles (90,000 sq km)
Population after implementation
of the Right Road to Peace Plan:
5,500,000

EGYPT

Eilat
■

SAUDI ARABIA

My Prayer for the Peace of Jerusalem

ALL THE RECEPTIONS ON THE WHITE HOUSE LAWN AND IN THE CAPITALS OF EUROPE HAVE NOT SUCCEEDED IN BRINGING ABOUT PEACE. ALL OF THE HIGH EXPECTATIONS RESULTED ONLY IN DEEP DISAPPOINTMENTS AND THE DEVASTATION OF LIVES LOST. THE MAIN RESULT OF THE OSLO ACCORDS HAS BEEN BLOODSHED. THE ROAD MAP AND ANY OTHER PROPOSED SOLUTION THAT FAILS TO RELY ON BIBLICAL JUSTICE AND THE COVENANT BETWEEN GOD AND HIS PEOPLE IS DOOMED TO FAILURE.

LET US PRAY (AS WE ARE COMMANDED TO) THAT THE GOD OF ABRAHAM, ISAAC, AND JACOB, OUR FATHER, OUR KING, THE GOD OF ISRAEL, THE LORD OF THE UNIVERSE WILL GRANT PEACE TO JERUSALEM. THAT HE WILL OPEN THE HEARTS AND EYES OF THE LEADERS OF ISRAEL, THE ARAB WORLD, AND THE UNITED STATES OF AMERICA. THAT THEY WILL WALK IN THE RIGHT ROAD TO PEACE FOR JERUSALEM AND NOT FIGHT AGAINST HIS HOLY LAND THAT HE PROMISED TO HIS PEOPLE ISRAEL AS AN ETERNAL POSSESSION.

GOD OF ISRAEL, LORD OF THE UNIVERSE, WE BESEECH YOU TO SHOW YOUR ALMIGHTY POWER AND CAST YOUR BLESSING AND PROTECTION OVER ALL THE DWELLERS OF YOUR LAND AND BRING PEACE TO JERUSALEM, YOUR HOLY CITY.

CHAPTER FIVE

I have invited Christian author and pastor, Dr. Larry Keefauver, to give an overview of God's Biblical covenant with the land.

THE COVENANT ESTABLISHED

By Dr. Larry Keefauver

While Joshua led Israel in the conquest of the land, the complete political and military conquest of the Land came under David and Solomon: David established Jerusalem as the capital, and his son Solomon built the Temple. To King David, God made this covenantal promise about the Promised Land:

But it happened that night that the word of the Lord came to Nathan, saying, "Go and tell My servant David, 'Thus says the Lord: "Would you build a house for Me to dwell in? For I have not dwelt in a house since the time that I brought the children of Israel up from Egypt, even to this day, but have moved about in a tent and in a tabernacle. Wherever I have moved about with all the children of Israel, have I ever spoken a word to anyone from the tribes of Israel, whom I commanded to shepherd My people Israel, saying, 'Why have you not built Me a house of cedar?' "

Now therefore, thus shall you say to My servant David, "Thus says the Lord of hosts: 'I took you from the sheepfold, from following the sheep, to be ruler over My people, over Israel. And I have been with you wherever you have gone, and have cut off all your enemies from before you, and have made you a great name, like the name of the great men who are on the earth. Moreover I will appoint a place for My people Israel, and will plant them, that they may dwell in a place of their own and move no more; nor shall the sons of wickedness oppress them anymore, as previously, since the time that I commanded judges to be over My people Israel, and have caused you to rest from all your enemies.' " [66]

The kingdom during the reign of King Solomon reflected the full extent of God's covenant promise to Israel. It fulfilled what God said to Jacob at Beth El.

The land on which you lie I will give to you and your descendants. Also your descendants shall be as the dust of the earth; you shall spread abroad to the west and the east, to the north and the south; and in you and in your seed all the families of the earth shall be blessed. Behold, I am with you and will keep you wherever you go, and will bring you back to this land; for I will not leave you until I have done what I have spoken to you. [67]

God made a covenant promise to Israel in Scripture. Let's explore more closely exactly what that covenant promise is and how Israel today fulfills God's covenant promise.

God's Covenant Promise to Israel

Ongoing and Forever —
The Land of Israel Belongs to the Jews

> I am the LORD God of Abraham your father and the God of Isaac; the land on which you lie I will give to you and your descendants. Also your descendants shall be as the dust of the earth; you shall spread abroad to the west and the east, to the north and the south; and in you and in your seed all the families of the earth shall be blessed. Behold, I am with you and will keep you wherever you go, and will bring you back to this land; for I will not leave you until I have done what I have spoken to you. [68]

A few years ago, a popular bumper sticker read, "God said it. I believe it. That settles it." While conventional wisdom may rest in what's popular and accepted by the majority, truth only rests with the

67. Genesis 28:13-15.
68. Genesis 28:13-15.

One who reveals it — the Living God. When God speaks, it's settled! The truth of God stands for all time, all people and in all situations. Whether "I believe it" is simply irrelevant. My opinion (and yours for that matter) simply doesn't matter in the eternal scheme of things. Here's bedrock truth: *God said it. That settles it!*

When God spoke to Jacob (Israel) and told him that the covenantal land of promise belonged to his descendants, the issue of possession and rights to occupy were settled for all time. God doesn't change His mind. God confirms in Malachi 3:6, "For I am the Lord, I do not change," and in Isaiah 14:24, God declares, "Surely, as I have thought, so it shall come to pass, And as I have purposed, so it shall stand."

Thus, it's significant that God not only initially reveals His covenant promise to Abram[69] concerning his descendants and the Land of Israel; but God also reiterates that covenant promise to Abraham's son, Isaac,[70] and to his grandson, Jacob.[71]

Why is this so significant? The covenant promise is made not just to Abraham and all his descendants, but specifically to the lineage of Isaac (not to Ishmael and his descendants nor to the sons born to Keturah nor to the descendants of Esau).

It is to Isaac and then Jacob, whom God names "Israel," [72] that "all the land of Canaan" is given by God in covenant. It's not simply the blessing of

69. Genesis 12:1, 13:14, 15:1-21, 17:1, 22:15.
70. Genesis 26:2.
71. Genesis 28:13.
72. Genesis 32:28.

Isaac that is bestowed upon Jacob instead of Esau. It's not a deception by a younger brother (Jacob) who "steals" a blind father's blessing intended for the older brother (Esau). The covenant right to the land comes not from what Jacob "stole." Rather it comes from the covenant-making living God, who is faithful and just — blessed be His name.

Examining two basic issues can help us understand God's covenant promise of the land to Israel.

- The nature and spiritual significance of covenant.
- The extent of Canaan, the physical land of promise.

God's Covenant Lasts!

Scholars and theologians may define covenant theology in different ways. Some understand that each successive covenant replaces the previous one. Others teach that each successive covenant builds upon the foundation laid by the previous covenants. While varying interpretations may take us in different directions, let's look at some basic truths.

God plainly states in establishing His covenant (i.e. Edenic, Adamic, Noahic, Abrahamic, Mosaic, Promised Land [Canaan] and Davidic) His terms and conditions. The format of God's covenant with His people is suzerainty covenant. As Supreme Sovereign, God the King dictates what the covenant is with its conditions — blessings and curses.

For example, God established the covenant in Eden with responsibilities for Adam and Eve. They were to be fruitful and multiply, to subdue and take dominion over the earth, and not to eat of the tree of the knowledge of good and evil. Obedience brought blessing. Disobedience brought the curse of death.

Literally to enter into covenant was "to cut a covenant" referring to a blood sacrifice which sealed the covenant. So, an animal sheds blood and dies, so that its skin can cover Adam and Eve in the Adamic covenant. Noah offers a sacrifice [73]; Abraham made sacrifices [74] and then he heard God's covenant reiterated in a dream.

Passover [75] becomes the sacrificial meal (the lamb's shed blood) and an eternal ordinance that commemorates God's deliverance from bondage and deliverance to the Promised Land. Thus God commanded Israel, "And you shall observe this thing as an ordinance for you and your sons forever. It will come to pass when you come to the land which the LORD will give you, just as He promised, that you shall keep this service" [76]

Then before Israel left the wilderness and entered the Promised Land, God reiterated His covenant promise to Moses, *"This is the land of which I swore to give Abraham, Isaac, and Jacob, saying, 'I will give it to your descendants.' I have caused you to see it with your eyes, but you shall not cross over there."* [77]

73. Genesis 8.
74. Genesis 15.
75. Exodus 12.
76. Exodus 12:24-26.
77. Deuteronomy 34:1-4.

To Joshua, God's covenant promise of the land is spoken, *"Now therefore, arise, go over this Jordan, you and all this people, to the land which I am giving to them — the children of Israel. Every place that the sole of your foot will tread upon I have given you, as I said to Moses. From the wilderness and this Lebanon as far as the great river, the River Euphrates, all the land of the Hittites, and to the Great Sea toward the going down of the sun, shall be your territory"* [78]

While Joshua failed to completely secure the land for the Israelites and ongoing wars and strife filled the era of the judges, under King David the land of covenant promise was politically and militarily secured and even expanded under King Solomon.

Interestingly, Jesus was continually asked if His kingdom was about land — the natural land of Palestine. Would He establish a political or military kingdom? Zealots hoped for a militant messiah who would come on the scene and vanquish the hated Roman occupiers. Probably Judas and Simon the Zealot were among Jesus' disciples who hoped for such an earthly kingdom.

But Jesus did not abrogate the covenant of promise concerning the Land of Israel as promised by God to the Jewish descendants of Abraham, Isaac, and Jacob. Jesus continually emphasized that His was a heavenly kingdom and that He would return as Messiah to rule and reign.

78. Joshua 1:2-3.

The early church understood prophetically that Jesus would return as Messiah to Mount of Olives, proceeding through the Eastern Gate of Jerusalem and ruling from the Temple Mount of Moriah, where Abraham laid out Isaac for sacrifice in obedience, where David bought the threshing floor for the Temple, and where Solomon ultimately built the Temple.

The author of Hebrews recognized the covenant land of promise when writing of Abraham:

> By faith Abraham obeyed when he was called to go out to the place which he would receive as an inheritance. And he went out, not knowing where he was going. By faith he dwelt in the land of promise as in a foreign country, dwelling in tents with Isaac and Jacob, the heirs with him of the same promise; for he waited for the city which has foundations, whose builder and maker is God. [79]

Simply put, God gave a covenant, unending and unbreakable promise to the descendants of Abraham, Isaac, and Jacob that they would have a land of promise. This covenant land of promise would be a perpetual inheritance for Israel, the Jewish people, for all of history. God's covenant promise of the land is irrevocable.

79. Hebrews 11:8-10. (emphasis added.)

What is the Land?

Biblically, the land of promise is called "Canaan" and "Palestine." It is defined not by national borders (such entities didn't exist in that period of history) but rather by geographical landmarks and groups of people that lived in the land. Living in the land never gave a people group the right to occupy or claim the land as their own. The Promised Land was always and always will be a gift from God to Israel — the natural descendants of Abraham, Isaac, and Jacob.

Spiritually, Christians have been grafted onto the tree of Israel.[80] God has never cast away His people, Israel.[81] The Old Testament prophecies foresaw the return of Israel from the nations of the earth.[82]

In Genesis 17:8, God promised to give Abraham's descendants "all the land of Canaan." The Bible prescribed Canaan as the place bounded "by the sea and along the banks of Jordan."[83] In Numbers 33:51 and Joshua 22:9, Canaan is described as the land west of the Jordan.[84] In Numbers 34, God sets the tribal boundaries for Israel of the Promised Land:

> Then the LORD spoke to Moses, saying, "Command the children of Israel, and say to them:

80. Romans 9:11.
81. Romans 11:2.
82. Ezekiel 28:25, 34:13, 36:24, 37:21-22. Isaiah 65:9-10. Jeremiah 23:3.
83. Numbers 13:29.
84. Genesis 12:5, 23:2&19, 28:1, 31:18, 35:6, 36:2, 37:1, 48:7. Exodus 15:15. Numbers 13:2. Joshua 14:1, 21:2. Psalms 135:11.

'When you come into the land of Canaan, this is the land that shall fall to you as an inheritance — the land of Canaan to its boundaries. Your southern border shall be from the Wilderness of Zin along the border of Edom; then your southern border shall extend eastward to the end of the Salt Sea; your border shall turn from the southern side of the Ascent of Akrabbim, continue to Zin, and be on the south of Kadesh Barnea; then it shall go on to Hazar Addar, and continue to Azmon; the border shall turn from Azmon to the Brook of Egypt, and it shall end at the Sea.

As for the western border, you shall have the Great Sea for a border; this shall be your western border.

And this shall be your northern border: From the Great Sea you shall mark out your border line to Mount Hor; from Mount Hor you shall mark out your border to the entrance of Hamath; then the direction of the border shall be toward Zedad; the border shall proceed to Ziphron, and it shall end at Hazar Enan. This shall be your northern border.

You shall mark out your eastern border from Hazar Enan to Shepham; the border shall go down from Shepham to Riblah on the east side of Ain; the border shall go down and reach to the eastern side of the Sea of Chinnereth; the border shall go down along the Jordan, and it shall end at the Salt Sea. This shall be your land with its surrounding boundaries.

Most simply today, God has given the covenant land of promise to the Israelites, the Jewish people who have descended from Abraham, Isaac, and Jacob. That land which Britain named Palestine and the Bible calls Canaan is bounded by the Sinai on the south, the Jordan on the east, the Mediterranean on the west, and Lebanon on the north. While this land was recognized by the U.N. in the creation of the state of Israel, during the war of 1948, Jordan invaded Israel and annexed portions of the west bank of the Jordan River and unilaterally made Palestinians living there citizens of Jordan — a citizenship Jordan revoked in 1988. In today's world, Israel belongs to the Jews, while the Palestinian state is properly Jordan.

In fact, in February 2003, twenty-two Palestinian unions in Judea, Samaria, and Gaza appealed secretly to Jordan's King Abdallah for his economic intervention in the "so-called" West Bank areas in spite of their knowledge of Arafat's strong objection to such machinations. These actions testify to the fact that the current mood would support the renewed link with Jordan and the dissolution of the Palestinian Authority.

The Covenant of the Land for Today

God's covenant promise of the land to the descendants of Abraham, Isaac, and Jacob is irrevocable. Israel's right to the land of Canaan ultimately rests not in U.N. mandates or resolutions, world opinion or courts, or military conflicts or conquests. Israel's rights to exist and occupy the land of Canaan rest in God's covenant promise established for thousands of years and perpetual until Messiah returns. It's imperative for all People of the Book, Old and New Testaments, to recognize what God has said as absolute truth and to consider the following steps:

- To obey God's imperative prayer command: "Pray for the peace of Jerusalem" as commanded in Psalm 122:6.

- To recognize God's covenant promise of the land of Canaan to the descendants of Abraham, Isaac and Jacob as detailed in Numbers 34.

- To join hands and stand with the nation of Israel in love and relationship to work in peace for the full establishment of God's covenant of land. As Christians we recognize that we do not support the root but that the *root (Israel) supports us.*[85]

---

85. Romans 11:18.

- To implement a just and right road to peace for all peoples living in Israel. This Right Road to Peace would correspond to God's covenant promise to Israel and realize historically what God has intended for millennia in the Promised Land.

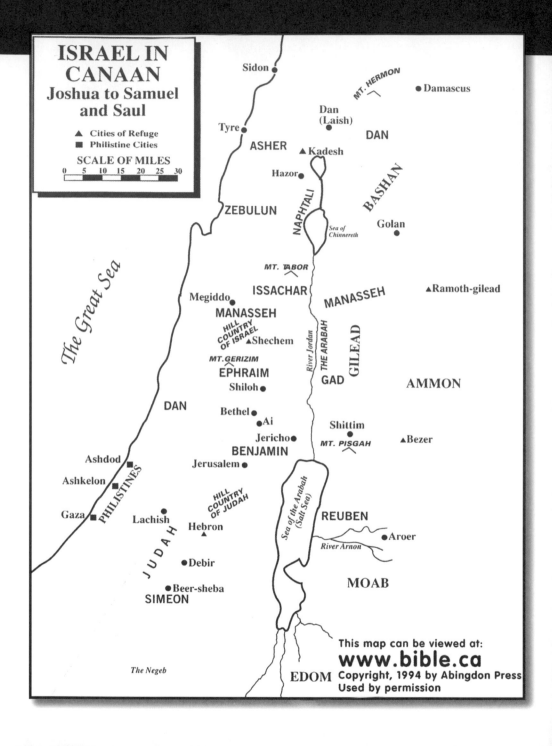

ISRAEL IN CANAAN
Joshua to Samuel and Saul

▲ Cities of Refuge
■ Philistine Cities

SCALE OF MILES
0   5   10 15 20 25 30

CHAPTER SIX

THE FINAL WORD:
WHAT WE CHRISTIANS CAN DO

Get Involved! Pray, Love, Commit & Become Part of a Movement!

By Dr. Larry Keefauver

We invite you to make the following covenant commitment to stand with Israel and then to send it in to Heartland to Heartland as you make a stand with Israel. How can Christians take a stand?

- Pray for the Peace of Jerusalem.
- Make a Covenant Commitment with Israel.
- Partner with Heartland to Heartland.

Pray for the Peace of Jerusalem

Too often we Christians waste time in prayer focusing on our wants instead of God's wants. Once we pray what He wants, we enter into the realm of imperative prayer. The living God of Abraham, Isaac, and Jacob has commanded us to pray for Jerusalem's peace. It is not an option, it is imperative!

Imperative prayer... what is it? The imperative of a verb is the command tense. In other words, when the imperative is used, action is demanded. Such is the case with God's imperative prayer in Scripture. Interestingly, only a handful of instances of imperative prayer can be found throughout the Bible. Their paucity gives pause to our intense study and dedicated obedience.

When God commands, *"PRAY!"* we must obey. In *imperative prayer,* God gets up close and personal. He gets in my face (i.e. face to face) and in your face and says, **"[You] pray!"**

In the Old Testament, the imperative form of prayer is focused and specific. A few characteristics of "imperative prayer" are:

- **Demanding**. God demands and commands; He doesn't suggest or merely invite us to pray.

- **Obeying**. The responsibility is upon us to obey. The seriousness of prayerlessness far exceeds simple neglect or forgetfulness; it's outright disobedience and rebellion. The subject of *imperative prayer* is "you." That makes the command personal, direct, and unremitting. So, I must think, "It's not what others are or are not doing; I must pray."

- **Ongoing**. To pray once isn't enough. Imperative prayer has an unending requirement upon us to be vigilant and persistent in prayer.

The essence of *imperative prayer* is this: God commands; you obey. That's it! No questions, discussion, or even dialogue. Growing up, my father had very few imperatives that he demanded of me. But those imperatives were non-negotiable, unchanging and always in effect. "Tell the truth." "Read your Bible and pray." "Do your chores." "Respect and obey your mother." "Listen and look at me when I talk to you." My feelings on a particular day or the extenuating conditions of a certain situation never changed these imperatives. They were "*musts.*"

The same is true of God. Imperative prayer in the Old Testament *must* be obeyed regardless of feelings, circumstance, or contrary opinions. Here it is: "*Pray for the peace of Jerusalem.*" [86]

Wait a moment. "What about the others?" Interestingly, there are no others in the Old Testament. In the New Testament, when properly clustered in synoptic form, there are only a few (eight) imperative prayer demands either on the lips of Jesus or from the Lord through the apostle Paul. [87]

While God demands certain prayer from a few specific Old Testament characters, His general, all-encompassing demand of prayer in the Old

86. Psalms 122:6.
87. (Mt. 6:5ff [Lk. 11:2ff], 9:38 [Lk. 10:2], 24:20 [Mk. 13:18], 26:41 [Mk. 14:38, Lk. 22:40ff]; Mk. 13:33 [Lk. 21:36]; Lk. 6:28; Eph. 6:18; 1 Thess. 5:17.

Testament upon all His people is singular, specific and straightforward: "Pray for the peace of Jerusalem."

The NIV and the NASB translations of this text understand the implied flow of the Hebrew. Once God demands prayer, He actually tells us *what* to pray:
"May they prosper who love you [Jerusalem].
May peace be within your walls,
and prosperity within your palaces. "[88]

In other words, God's singular, pointed, and specific imperative for prayer before Messiah comes in the new covenant is this: *pray for Jerusalem's peace and pray this way!* No ifs. No buts. No excuses. No time off. No exceptions.

So, are you? If not, when will you start? Will you be consistent, persistent, perserverant, and obedient in praying for Jerusalem's peace? I am under conviction. Are you?

---

88. Psalms 122:6b-7 NASB.

Make a Covenant Commitment of Love for Israel

The pledge cards that follow speak of relationship, of loving our older brother, the Jewish people. We Christians must stand with them as People of the Book. We must demonstrate to them the love of the Father.

What is it that marks us? Jesus said,

*"By this all will know that you are My disciples,
if you have love for one another."*[89]

As Christians, we believe that Jesus prophesied that during the end times, the love of many would wax cold. We cannot allow that to happen in our relationship with Israel. To love God is to love the descendants of Abraham, Isaac and Jacob and to love Jerusalem: *"May they prosper who love you [Jerusalem]."*[90]

We Christians know God's love for Jerusalem and for His people brings a blessing to all who bless them. The whole book of Hosea declares God's unchanging love for His child, Israel.[91] Through the prophet Isaiah, Almighty God declares:

> Rejoice with Jerusalem,
> And be glad with her, all you who love her;
> Rejoice for joy with her, all you who mourn

89. John 13:35.
90. Psalms 122:6.
91. cf. Hosea 11:1.

for her;
That you may feed and be satisfied
With the consolation of her bosom,
That you may drink deeply and be delighted
With the abundance of her glory.

For thus says the LORD:

"Behold, I will extend peace to her like a river,
And the glory of the Gentiles like a flowing
stream.
Then you shall feed;
On her sides shall you be carried,
And be dandled on her knees.
As one whom his mother comforts,
So I will comfort you;
And you shall be comforted in Jerusalem." [92]

As a Christian, sign the Pledge to Preserve Israel on the next page. Take a stand publicly. Profess your love for Israel!

---

92. Isaiah 66:10-13.

Pledge to Preserve Israel
MY PERSONAL COVENANT WITH GOD

THERE BESIDE HIM STOOD THE LORD, AND HE SAID: "I AM THE LORD, THE GOD OF YOUR FATHER ABRAHAM AND THE GOD OF ISAAC. I WILL GIVE YOU AND YOUR DESCENDANTS THE LAND ON WHICH YOU ARE LYING. YOUR DESCENDANTS WILL BE LIKE THE DUST OF THE EARTH, AND YOU WILL SPREAD OUT TO THE WEST AND TO THE EAST, TO THE NORTH AND TO THE SOUTH. ALL PEOPLES ON EARTH WILL BE BLESSED THROUGH YOU AND YOUR OFFSPRING. I AM WITH YOU AND WILL WATCH OVER YOU WHEREVER YOU GO, AND I WILL BRING YOU BACK TO THIS LAND. I WILL NOT LEAVE YOU UNTIL I HAVE DONE WHAT I HAVE PROMISED YOU."

Genesis 28:13-15

WHEREAS
I believe in the word of God as set out
in the Holy Bible;

AND WHEREAS
the Bible records that the Lord God granted
the Holy Land, Israel,
and its eternal capital Jerusalem,
to the Jewish people as an inheritance forever;

AND WHEREAS
this Covenant with Israel was proclaimed
and marked at holy sites in Beth El, Hebron, Shechem, and
Jerusalem, the heartland of Israel;

NOW THEREFORE, I

Name _____

Hereby Pledge

to act in accordance with the will of God to preserve Israel's sovereignty over the Holy Land and to prevent the alienation of Israel's Biblical heartland, Judea and Samaria, and it's eternal capital Jerusalem, from the State of Israel and the Jewish people.

Sign _____   Date _____

Tear Out and Put in Your Bible

…tian leaders who have signed the pledge to preserve Israel:

KAY ARTHUR
CEO, Precept Ministries

REV. TOMMY BARNETT
Pastor, Phoenix 1st Assembly
Co-Pastor, Los Angeles Dream Center

GARY BAUER
President, American Values

PASTOR RAY BENTLEY
Maranatha Chapel

REV. JERRY FALWELL
Chancellor, Liberty University

LEO GIOVINETTI
Pastor, Mission Valley Christian Fellowship

DR. JOHN C. & DIANA HAGEE
Pastors, Cornerstone Church,
CEO, Global Evangelism Television Inc

DR. JACK HAYFORD
President, International Foursquare Church
Chancellor, King's College & Seminary

MICHAEL LITTLE
President, CBN

PASTORS GEORGE & CHERYL MORRISON
Faith Bible Chapel

GLENN PLUMMER
Board of Directors, NRB
Pastor, Ambassadors for Christ Church

STEPHEN STRANG
Publisher, Charisma Magazine

REV. THOMAS TRASK
General Superintendent
Assemblies of God USA

PASTOR LASALLE VAUGHN
New Life Christian Center

DR. PAUL L. WALKER
Assistant General Overseer
Church of God International, Cleveland,TN

What can I do to fulfill my pledge?

1. **Pray for the Peace of Jerusalem.**
2. **Call and write your congressman, senator, and President Bush.**
3. **Ask your pastor if he would speak about the pledge to your congregation**
4. **Write an article about the pledge for your church bulletin.**
5. **Ask your pastor to sign the pledge on behalf of your church.**
6. **Write a letter to the editor of your local newspaper.**
7. **Come visit Israel.**
8. **Make a donation to Heartland to Heartland.**
9. **Start a Heartland to Heartland chapter where you live.**
10. **Read "God's Covenant with Israel" by Member of Knesset Rabbi Elon.**
11. **Discuss the pledge with family and friends.**
12. **Call and write your congressman, senator, and President Bush, again and ask what has been done.**

Visit **www.heartlandtoheartland.org** *for more details.*

There beside him stood the LORD, and he said: "I am the LORD, the God of your father Abraham and the God of Isaac. I will give you and your descendants the land on which you are lying. Your descendants will be like the dust of the earth, and you will spread out to the west and to the east, to the north and to the south. All peoples on earth will be blessed through you and your offspring. I am with you and will watch over you wherever you go, and I will bring you back to this land. I will not leave you until I have done what I have promised you." Genesis 28:13-15

WHEREAS I believe in the word of God as set out in the Holy Bible;

AND WHEREAS the Bible records that the Lord God granted the Holy Land, Israel, and its eternal capital Jerusalem, to the Jewish people as an inheritance forever;

AND WHEREAS this Covenant with Israel was proclaimed and marked at holy sites in Bethel, Hebron, Shechem, and Jerusalem, the heartland of Israel;

NOW THEREFORE, I, _____,

HEREBY PLEDGE to act in accordance with the will of God to preserve Israel's sovereignty over the Holy Land and to prevent the alienation of Israel's Biblical heartland, Judea and Samaria, and it's eternal capital Jerusalem, from the State of Israel and the Jewish people.

Name: _____ *E-mail* _____

Address: _____

Church: _____ *Pastor* _____

State _____ *Zip code:* _____

Congressional District: _____

Comments: _____

_____

Mail to:
Jerusalem Office   *Washington D.C. Office*
Heartland to Heartland   **Heartland to Heartland**
Derech Shechem 12   1718 M St. NW # 260
Jerusalem, 91000   Washington, DC 20036
P.O.B 1522 ISRAEL   USA

HEARTLAND
TO HEARTLAND

(H2H)

Heartland to Heartland is a bilateral organization bringing together Christians and Jews, in an alliance based on Biblical values, to keep the Biblical heartland of Israel, Judea, and Samaria, under the sovereignty of the State of Israel, and so prevent the creation of an Arab terrorist state in the heart of the Holy Land. Heartland to Heartland believes that the Judeo-Christian values, which have their source in the Bible, arc the foundation of the friendship and alliance between America and Israel. Heartland to Heartland is jointly managed from offices in Jerusalem and Washington D.C.

We are reaching the end game in the battle between Jews and Arabs for control of Israel's heartland. The current Israeli government has forced through the disengagement legislation for Gaza and Northern Samaria, and it is clear it is preparing to surrender the bulk of Judea and Samaria, as well. This is not the will of the people of Israel, who remain as faithful to their Biblical covenant with God as they have through the ages.

Israel's only hope now is to rally the Christian faithful in America to petition President Bush, through Congress, to oppose the dismemberment of Israel and so keep faith with the Biblical covenant between God and the children of Israel.

Heartland to Heartland is dedicated to mobilizing grass roots Christian support for the proposition that Judea and Samaria are integral parts of the land granted to the Jewish people by God's covenant with the children of Israel. America's Christians, and they alone, have the influence, through their representatives in the House and Senate, to give the President the backing he needs to resist international pressure and do what he would like to do in any event — prevent the creation of another terrorist state.

Through God's grace, the President and the Republican Party have won an unprecedented victory in the recent elections, which has made American support for the preservation of the territorial integrity of the State of Israel possible. God has given us the opportunity to keep faith with the Biblical covenant. It remains only for the faithful to do their part.

Jerusalem Office:
Heartland to Heartland
Derech Shechem 12
Jerusalem, 91000
P.O.B 1522
ISRAEL

Washington D.C. Office:
Heartland to Heartland
1718 M St. NW # 260
Washington, DC 20036
USA

Appendix 1

About the Author
Rabbi Binyamin (Benny) Elon

Member of Knesset Rabbi Binyamin Elon has served two terms as Tourism Minister of the State of Israel. He is the chairman of the Moledet Party, and a member of the Christian Allies Caucus.
Born in 1954, Benny Elon is a seventh-generation Jerusalemite, residing in the community of Beth El for the last twenty-two years. He has rabbinic ordination and is married to popular newspaper columnist and author Emuna Elon. They are the proud parents of six and grandparents of eight.

Rabbi Elon has been active in Israeli public affairs for over a decade. Before that he served as Rabbi of Kibbutz Shluhot near the Sea of Galilee. He established the prestigious "Beth Oroth" Rabbinical college on the Mount of Olives in Jerusalem. Most prominently, he has been working to preserve the unity of Jerusalem as Israel's undivided and eternal capital and the integrity of Judea and Samaria, Israel's heartland. He is well known, not only for his political acumen, but also for his ability to translate his sound, ideological philosophies into facts on the ground.

Jerusalem continues to be strengthened by his efforts to reclaim Jewish neighborhoods in all parts of the city, rendering any division of Israel's capital untenable. Rabbi Elon works to create the continuity of Jewish presence in east and west Jerusalem to preserve united Jerusalem as the eternal capital of Israel.

Benny Elon is well known in Israel as an influential religious leader, and as a prominent activist on behalf of Jewish settlement in Judea, Samaria and Gaza (YESHA). He fights for annexation of YESHA into the State of Israel.

He has striven to unite the right-wing parties under one larger faction — the National Union, which today comprises seven out of the 120 Members of the Knesset.

Another focal point of his activities is to strengthen Israel's political standing in the western world and specifically in the United States. For this purpose he has developed relationships with the Jewish communities worldwide, in addition to which he has put much effort into establishing strong relations with the Christian community.

He served in the 14th and 15th Knessets and was awarded the "Distinguished Service" citation by his political peers. His parliamentary duties have included membership of the Foreign Affairs and Defense Committee, Law and Justice, and the Committee for the Appointment of Judges.

Appendix 2

Key Prophetic Scriptures about Israel

These texts demonstrate Biblically that God has entered into everlasting covenant for the descendants of Abraham, Isaac, and Jacob to possess and occupy the Promised Land. As you pray for the Peace of Jerusalem, read these passages.

Genesis 28:13-15
God's Covenant Promise of the Land to Abraham, Isaac and Jacob

"I am the LORD God of Abraham your father and the God of Isaac; the land on which you lie I will give to you and your descendants. Also your descendants shall be as the dust of the earth; you shall spread abroad to the west and the east, to the north and the south; and in you and in your seed all the families of the earth shall be blessed. Behold, I am with you and will keep you wherever you go, and will bring you back to this land; for I will not leave you until I have done what I have spoken to you."

Deuteronomy 30:1-6
Israel is gathered back again from among the nations into the Promised Land

"Now it shall come to pass, when all these things come upon you, the blessing and the curse which I have set before you, and you call them to mind among all the nations where the LORD your God drives you, and you return to the LORD your God and obey His voice, according to all that I command you today, you and your children, with all your heart and with all your soul, that the LORD your God will bring you back from captivity, and have compassion on you, and gather you again from all the nations where the LORD your God has scattered you. If any of you are driven out to the farthest parts under heaven, from there the LORD your God will gather you, and from there He will bring you. Then the LORD your God will bring you to the land which your fathers possessed, and you shall possess it. He will prosper you and multiply you more than your fathers. And the LORD your God will circumcise your heart and the heart of your descendants, to love the LORD your God with all your heart and with all your soul, that you may live."

Isaiah 27:12-13
God promised to restore Israel

"And it shall come to pass in that day
That the LORD will thresh,
From the channel of the River to the Brook of Egypt;
And you will be gathered one by one,
O you children of Israel.
'So it shall be in that day:
The great trumpet will be blown;
They will come, who are about to perish in the land of Assyria,
And they who are outcasts in the land of Egypt,
And shall worship the LORD in the holy mount at Jerusalem."

Isaiah 43:5-6
Isaiah foretold of the worldwide return of Israel to the Promised Land

"Fear not, for I am with you;
I will bring your descendants from the east,
And gather you from the west;
I will say to the north, 'Give them up!'
And to the south, 'Do not keep them back!'
Bring My sons from afar,
And My daughters from the ends of the earth."

Jeremiah 23:3-6
The House of Israel would be re-gathered

"But I will gather the remnant of My flock out of all countries where I have driven them, and bring them back to their folds; and they shall be fruitful and increase. I will set up shepherds over them who will feed them; and they shall fear no more, nor be dismayed, nor shall they be lacking," says the LORD.

"Behold, the days are coming," says the LORD,
"That I will raise to David a Branch of righteousness;
A King shall reign and prosper,
And execute judgment and righteousness in the earth.
In His days Judah will be saved,
And Israel will dwell safely;
Now this is His name by which He will be called:

"Therefore, behold, the days are coming," says the LORD, "that they shall no longer say, 'As the LORD lives who brought up the children of Israel from the land of Egypt,' but, 'As the LORD lives who brought up and led the descendants of the house of Israel from the north country and from all the countries where I had driven them.' And they shall dwell in their own land."

Jeremiah 32:36-37
Israel would survive Babylonian rule and return home in an everlasting covenant

"Now therefore, thus says the LORD, the God of Israel, concerning this city of which you say, 'It shall be delivered into the hand of the king of Babylon by the sword, by the famine, and by the pestilence: Behold, I will gather them out of all countries where I have driven them in My anger, in My fury, and in great wrath; I will bring them back to this place, and I will cause them to dwell safely. They shall be My people, and I will be their God; then I will give them one heart and one way, that they may fear Me forever, for the good of them and their children after them. And I will make an everlasting covenant with them, that I will not turn away from doing them good; but I will put My fear in their hearts so that they will not depart from Me. Yes, I will rejoice over them to do them good, and I will assuredly plant them in this land, with all My heart and with all My soul.'"

Ezekiel 20:34
God promised that the Jews would return from other nations to the Land of Israel

"I will bring you out from the peoples and gather you out of the countries where you are scattered, with a mighty hand, with an outstretched arm, and with fury poured out."

Ezekiel 34:13
God gathers Israel back to their own land

"And I will bring them out from the peoples and gather them from the countries, and will bring them to their own land; I will feed them on the mountains of Israel, in the valleys and in all the inhabited places of the country."

Ezekiel 36:24
Israel would be re-gathered by God

"For I will take you from among the nations, gather you out of all countries, and bring you into your own land."

Amos 9:14-15
Jacob's descendants would regain control of Israel

"I will bring back the captives of My people Israel;
They shall build the waste cities and inhabit them;
They shall plant vineyards and drink wine from them;
They shall also make gardens and eat fruit from them."

"I will plant them in their land,
And no longer shall they be pulled up
From the land I have given them,"
Says the LORD your God.

Zechariah 8:7-8
Zechariah prophesied Israel's return to Jerusalem

"Thus says the LORD of hosts:
Behold, I will save My people from the land of the
east And from the land of the west;
I will bring them back,
And they shall dwell in the midst of Jerusalem.
They shall be My people
And I will be their God,
In truth and righteousness."

THE SOVEREIGN NATION OF ISRAEL

Genesis 15:18-21
Abraham's descendants would have their own country

"On the same day the LORD made a covenant with Abram, saying: To your descendants I have given this land, from the river of Egypt to the great river, the River Euphrates — the Kenites, the Kenezzites, the Kadmonites, the Hittites, the Perizzites, the Rephaim, the Amorites, the Canaanites, the Girgashites, and the Jebusites."

Genesis 35:9-15
Jacob's descendants would inherit the Land of Israel

"Then God appeared to Jacob again, when he came from Padan Aram, and blessed him. And God said to him, 'Your name is Jacob; your name shall not be called Jacob anymore, but Israel shall be your name.' So He called his name Israel. Also God said to him: 'I am God Almighty. Be fruitful and multiply; a nation and a company of nations shall proceed from you, and kings shall come from your body. The land which I gave Abraham and Isaac I give to you; and to your descendants after you I give this land.' Then God went up from him in the place where He talked with him. So Jacob set up a pillar in the place where He talked with him, a pillar of stone; and he poured a drink offering on it, and he poured oil on it. And Jacob called the name of the place where God spoke with him, Bethel."

Isaiah 66:7-8
Isaiah spoke of Israel being reborn in one day

"Before she was in labor, she gave birth;
Before her pain came,
She delivered a male child.
Who has heard such a thing?
Who has seen such things?
Shall the earth be made to give birth in one day?
Or shall a nation be born at once?
For as soon as Zion was in labor,

She gave birth to her children.
'Shall I bring to the time of birth, and not cause delivery?' says the LORD.
'Shall I who cause delivery shut up the womb?' says your God.
Rejoice with Jerusalem,
And be glad with her, all you who love her;
Rejoice for joy with her, all you who mourn for her;
That you may feed and be satisfied
With the consolation of her bosom,
That you may drink deeply and be delighted
With the abundance of her glory."

Jeremiah 16:14-15
The Israel would be brought back to the land promised to their forefathers

" 'Therefore behold, the days are coming,' says the LORD, 'that it shall no more be said, "The LORD lives who brought up the children of Israel from the land of Egypt," but, "The LORD lives who brought up the children of Israel from the land of the north and from all the lands where He had driven them." For I will bring them back into their land which I gave to their fathers.' "

Ezekiel 11:14-17
Israel would be re-gathered and dwell in Israel as their country, again

"Again the word of the LORD came to me, saying, 'Son of man, your brethren, your relatives, your countrymen, and all the house of Israel in its entirety, are those about whom the inhabitants of Jerusalem have said, "Get far away from the LORD; this land has been given to us as a possession." Therefore say, 'Thus says the Lord GOD: "Although I have cast them far off among the Gentiles, and although I have scattered them among the countries, yet I shall be a little sanctuary for them in the countries where they have gone." 'Therefore say, 'Thus says the Lord GOD: "I will gather you from the peoples, assemble you from the countries where you have been scattered, and I will give you the Land of Israel.' "

Ezekiel 37:1-23
New life as a nation would be breathed into Israel

"The hand of the LORD came upon me and brought me out in the Spirit of the LORD, and set me down in the midst of the valley; and it was full of bones. Then He caused me to pass by them all around, and behold, there were very many in the open valley; and indeed they were very dry. And He said to me, 'Son of man, can these bones live?' So I answered, 'O Lord GOD, You know.' Again He said to me, 'Prophesy to these bones, and say to them, 'O dry bones, hear the word of the LORD! Thus says the Lord GOD to these bones: "Surely I will cause breath to enter into you, and you shall live. I will put sinews on you and bring flesh upon you, cover you with skin and put breath in you; and you shall live. Then you shall know that I am the LORD."

"So I prophesied as I was commanded; and as I prophesied, there was a noise, and suddenly a rattling; and the bones came together, bone to bone. Indeed, as I looked, the sinews and the flesh came upon them, and the skin covered them over; but there was no breath in them."

Also He said to me, "Prophesy to the breath, prophesy, son of man, and say to the breath, Thus says the Lord GOD: "Come from the four winds, O breath, and breathe on these slain, that they may live." "So I prophesied as He commanded me, and breath came into them, and they lived, and stood upon their feet, an exceedingly great army."

"Then He said to me, "Son of man, these bones are the whole house of Israel. They indeed say, 'Our bones are dry, our hope is lost, and we ourselves are cut off!' Therefore prophesy and say to them, Thus says the Lord GOD: "Behold, O My people, I will open your graves and cause you to come up from your graves, and bring you into the Land of Israel. Then you shall know that I am the LORD, when I have opened your graves, O My people, and brought you up from your graves. I will put My Spirit in you, and you shall live, and I will place you in your own land. Then you shall know that I, the LORD, have spoken it and performed it," says the LORD.

Again the word of the LORD came to me, saying, "As for you, son of man, take a stick for yourself and write on it: 'For Judah and for the children of Israel, his companions.' Then take another stick and write on it, 'For Joseph, the stick of Ephraim, and for all the house of Israel, his companions.' Then join them one to another for yourself into one stick, and they will become one in your hand."

"And when the children of your people speak to you, saying, 'Will you not show us what you mean by these?' — say to them, 'Thus says the Lord GOD: "Surely I will take the stick of Joseph, which is in the hand of Ephraim, and the tribes of Israel, his companions; and I will join them with it, with the stick of Judah, and make them one stick, and they will be one in My hand." ' And the sticks on which you write will be in your hand before their eyes.

"Then say to them, 'Thus says the Lord GOD: "Surely I will take the children of Israel from among the nations, wherever they have gone, and will gather them from every side and bring them into their own land; and I will make them one nation in the land, on the mountains of Israel; and one king shall be king over them all; they shall no longer be two nations, nor shall they ever be divided into two kingdoms again. They shall not defile themselves anymore with their idols, nor with their detestable things, nor with any of their transgressions; but

I will deliver them from all their dwelling places in which they have sinned, and will cleanse them. Then they shall be My people, and I will be their God!"

PRESERVATION OF ISRAEL

Counting Abraham's descendants would be like counting the stars.

Genesis 15:5

"Then He brought him outside and said, 'Look now toward heaven, and count the stars if you are able to number them.' And He said to him, 'So shall your descendants be.'"

Leviticus 26:3, 7-8.
Israel's army would be disproportionately powerful

"If you walk in My statutes and keep My commandments, and perform them, then I will give you rain in its season, the land shall yield its produce, and the trees of the field shall yield their fruit.
Your threshing shall last till the time of vintage, and the vintage shall last till the time of sowing; you shall eat your bread to the full, and dwell in your land safely.

I will give peace in the land, and you shall lie down,
and none will make you afraid;
I will rid the land of evil beasts,
and the sword will not go through your land.
You will chase your enemies, and they shall fall by
the sword before you.
Five of you shall chase a hundred, and a hundred
of you shall put ten thousand to flight;
your enemies shall fall by the sword before you."

Leviticus 26:44
God will keep His covenant with Israel

"But if they confess their iniquity and the iniquity
of their fathers, with their unfaithfulness in which
they were unfaithful to Me, and that they also have
walked contrary to Me,
and that I also have walked contrary to them and
have brought them into the land of their enemies;
if their uncircumcised hearts are humbled, and
they accept their guilt — then I will remember My
covenant with Jacob, and My covenant with Isaac
and My covenant with Abraham I will remember;
I will remember the land.
The land also shall be left empty by them, and
will enjoy its sabbaths while it lies desolate without
them;
they will accept their guilt, because they despised
My judgments and because their soul abhorred My
statutes.

Yet for all that, when they are in the land of their enemies, I will not cast them away, nor shall I abhor them, to utterly destroy them and break My covenant with them;
for I am the LORD their God.
But for their sake I will remember the covenant of their ancestors, whom I brought out of the land of Egypt in the sight of the nations, that I might be their God:
I am the LORD."

Isaiah 66:22
Isaiah said God would preserve Israel

"For as the new heavens and the new earth
Which I will make shall remain before Me," says the LORD,
"So shall your descendants and your name remain."

Jeremiah 30:11
God will save Israel and destroy its enemies

"For I am with you, says the LORD, to save you;
Though I make a full end of all nations where I have scattered you,
Yet I will not make a complete end of you.
But I will correct you in justice,
And will not let you go altogether unpunished."

Jeremiah 31:35-36

The people of Israel will never cease to be a nation of people

"Thus says the LORD,
Who gives the sun for a light by day,
The ordinances of the moon and the stars for a
light by night,
Who disturbs the sea,
And its waves roar
(The LORD of hosts is His name):

"If those ordinances depart
From before Me, says the LORD,
Then the seed of Israel shall also cease
From being a nation before Me forever."

Jeremiah 46:28

Enemies of Israel will cease to be nations

"Do not fear, O Jacob My servant," says the
LORD,
"For I am with you;
For I will make a complete end of all the nations
To which I have driven you,
But I will not make a complete end of you.
I will rightly correct you,
For I will not leave you wholly unpunished."

Zechariah 8:13
The people of Israel would be persecuted, but preserved

"And it shall come to pass
That just as you were a curse among the nations,
O house of Judah and house of Israel,
So I will save you, and you shall be a blessing.
Do not fear,
Let your hands be strong."

ISRAEL IS RESTORED ACCORDING TO GOD'S COVENANT PROMISES

The following is a collection of text references that speak of the restoration of Israel; many of these texts have already been quoted but this list speaks of the many ways Israel's restoration would be evidenced. We are witnesses today in Israel of the fulfillment of these prophetic promises of the Living God.

Deuteronomy 30:3-5
The fortunes of the people of Israel would be restored

Isaiah 27:12-13
God promised to restore Israel

Isaiah 35:1-2
Isaiah foretold the restoration of Israel

Isaiah 41:18-20
Trees would flourish again in a desolate Israel

Isaiah 43:5-6
Isaiah foretold of the worldwide return of the House of Israel to the Land of Israel

Isaiah 51:3
Israel's deserts will become like the Garden of Eden

Jeremiah 32:44
Jeremiah said the children of Israel would buy back land

Ezekiel 36:8-10
Israel would be restored and repopulated

Ezekiel 36:11
Ezekiel prophesied prosperity for a restored Israel

Ezekiel 36:33-35
Israel would be rebuilt and resettled

Ezekiel 37:10-14
Israel would be brought back to life

Ezekiel 37:15-19
The people of Israel again would be a united people

Hosea 3:4-5
The people of Israel would live many days without a king

Joel 2:22
Israel would again become a prosperous land

Amos 9:11,13
The ruins of Israel would be rebuilt

Amos 9:14-15
Jacob's descendants would regain control of Israel

Micah 7:8-11
Israel would rise again

Zechariah 8:12
Israel's land would again become fruitful

Appendix 3

A Report From
Palestinian Media Watch

Palestinian Media Watch has played a vital role in the current conflict by providing insight into Palestinian thought and intentions. This report is included because I feel that it is so important to know what is being said in the Arab world about Israel, America, and the "People of the Book."

Palestinian Media Watch was established in 1996 to gain an understanding of Palestinian society through the monitoring of the Palestinian Arabic language media and schoolbooks. PMW analyzes Palestinian Authority [PA] culture and society from numerous perspectives, including studies on summer camps, poetry, schoolbooks, religious ideology, crossword puzzles, and many more. PMW has been playing the critical role of documenting the contradictions between the images that the Palestinians present to the world in English and the messages to their own people in Arabic. The world's view of the Palestinian Authority, to a significant degree, is the result of PMW research. For more information please visit the web site at: **www.pmw.org.il.** Itamar Marcus is director of PMW.

PA HISTORIANS:

**Israel's Biblical History is Actually
Arab Muslim History**
by Itamar Marcus, August 8, 2004.

Introduction

On an educational program on PA TV, two senior Palestinian Authority [PA] historians went
to great lengths to deny ancient Jewish history
and erase the Jewish connection to the Land
of Israel. At the same time they describe an ancient Palestinian - Arab history, creating a historical connection to the land that never existed.

Two central components of this Palestinian myth
consist of turning biblical Israelites into Muslim -
Arabs, while teaching that the Palestinians are the
descendents of the biblical Canaanites, who are
also turned into Arabs. With both the Canaanites
and Israelites becoming Arabs and the religion of
ancient Israel becoming Islam, the PA takes au-
thentic Jewish history, documented by thousands of
years of continuous literature, crosses out the word
"Jewish" and replaces it with the word "Arab."

This creative historical revisionism is not new in
the PA. Denying the thousands of years of Jewish
connection to the Land of Israel, coupled with the
invention of a "Palestinian" history of thousands
of years, has always been of supreme importance
to the Palestinian Authority. The PA is struggling

with the challenge of creating a Palestinian national identity when no Palestinian national history exists. Even the term "Palestine" historically had nothing to do with Arab identity, and most of the population only migrated in the last century after the improved living conditions and work opportunities brought about by the Zionist movement.

Thus, incessant denial of Israel's history and right to exist, and the invention of a Palestinian history have been backbones of PA indoctrination and education for years.

In a broadcast on PA TV, the following are some of the main points of the "history"

- The Hebrews of the Bible have no connection to the Jews today.
- The Hebrews of the Bible were Arabs.
- The Prophets of the Bible were Muslims.
- Biblical King Solomon was a Muslim Prophet.
- Solomon's Temple was not built by Israelites but by Arab Canaanites.
- The Canaanites are the forefathers of the Palestinians.
- The Bible is a collection of legends based on what Jews imagined and not on history.
- The Jews today are descendents of a 13th Century Khazar tribe with no history in the Land of Israel.
- The location of the Temple Mount in Jerusalem is a Zionist invention.
- Zionism is Racism.

The following are selections from the discussion on PA TV:

The historians:

Dr. Jarir Al-Qidwah, Head of the PA Public Library and Arafat's Advisor on Education.

Dr. Issam Sissalem, Senior Historian and Educational TV host, former head of History Dept. of PA University.

Moderator: Mohammed Albaz
PA TV, Aug. 2, 2004

Albaz: "Where did the story of Solomon's Temple come from?"

Al-Qidwa: "Solomon's Temple, I believe, was built by the Canaanites who were the neighbors of the Israelis, the Israelites... I want to state several words clearly: the Bible became an archival document, not representing what the Israelis and the first Jews were, but what they thought they were, what they imagined. The Temple is the fruit of their imagination. In any case, when our nation or our Canaanite forefathers came to Palestine, they built the Temple and a temple in Jerusalem."

Sissalem: "We, as the Palestinian nation fighting for its freedom and liberation, must not focus too much attention on these false [Biblical] legends. The history of our land continues more than ten thousand years. The land of battles and wars, [many] armies, tribes, and commanders came through. I want to point out that we should not focus much on what is called the [Biblical] Hebrew tribes, who are in fact Bedouin Arab tribes. There is no connection between them and these Khazar Jews [of Israel today]. Those [Hebrew - Arab] tribes were erased and ceased to exist and no traces were left of them. That group did not have a pure religion. They claimed that Solomon, may he rest in peace, built the Temple. Does the land testify to this? Solomon was a prophet and we see him as a Muslim and part of our [Islamic] heritage. There is no historical text that proves the existence [of the temple] or that it has a real history other than the Bible, and the Bible as we have previously mentioned and was written based on ancient legends."

"The Quran came directly from the Prophet [Muhammad]... while supporting all that preceded it in the [Biblical] Prophetic inscriptions, that, as you noted, appeared in the Quran as Muslims believing in the one and only God, and these [the Hebrew prophets of the Bible] are part of our [Muslim] heritage. They have no connection to the Imperialistic Settlement Jews [Israelis] and nor to those that were destroyed."

Al-Qidwa: "The Jewish presence in Palestine and Jerusalem ended approximately in the year 70, when Titus utterly destroyed the Second Temple of Herod."

Sissalem: "When the Zionist movement started to set in motion the Imperialist Settlement plan, it tried to base itself in the Biblical legends, as we said The Bible expresses a tradition of legends, that has no connection to history."

Viewer calls studio: "We say that when the Israelites... migrated to America. But the World Zionist Movement and the Free Masons drove them, while distorting the Bible and the Protocols of the Elders of Zion and the newly prepared Bible, drove them to come here [Israel] and these [the Jews] are the foreign invaders that will pass as the others passed, Allah willing."

Al-Qidwa: "Allah willing."

Sissalem: "Allah willing."

Albaz: "Allah willing."

Caller continues: "And Palestine will be for them a cemetery, Allah willing."

Al-Qidwa: "Zionism is a racist movement that mixes or wears a religious cloak, and it is false, but it mixes the nation and religion, like the mixture of the Jews. The Jews are a religion and not a race. The peculiar mixture we mentioned in the beginning is meant to follow the historical roots of the Bible, establishing a Jewish state in Palestine, and a so-called Jewish temple in the place of [Islamic] Al Haram."

Al-Qidwa: "The issue of the temple is a Zionist innovation. No one said that the temple that was built in Jerusalem, neither the Canaanite nor Roman, no one said that it was in the place of the [Islamic] Al Haram."

Al-Qidwa: "These Jews, [after being conquered by Rome] were dispersed ... among many nations. The last, after many hundreds of years, the Khazar Jews, [are the ones] who live in Palestine [i.e., Israel] today. When these people started to write the Bible they found that it was written in a [foreign] language... When they reached Palestine they had no knowledge or culture."

Albaz: "And without any historical or other link [to the land]."

Al-Qidwa: "And without any historical or other link... At first they were Shepherds. When they needed agricultural instruments, they went to the Canaanite cities to buy metal rods and knives and other things."

Sissalem: "And about the Jews of Khazar... they had a state [in the Kavkaz (Caucasia)] and it was destroyed by the Vladimir Family and the Mongolian attack, that invaded them in the 13th century. They dispersed in seclusion in ghettos, in what is called Russia, Ukraine, and Poland, and came to us [to Israel] in the 19th century, with false Zionist claims based on legends."

Appendix 4

The Biblical Bond as the Basis of International Law: The Legal Status of Israel and the Settlements

The following essay deals with the legality of Israel, including Judea and Samaria, from an international, judicial, legal, and secular perspective. There is a saying that if you repeat a lie long enough, people will begin to believe it. That is exactly what has happened to Israel in the eyes of the world. Revisionist historians have changed the memory of many nations who now side against Israel. The summary of the history behind the creation of the modern state of Israel is included here because these facts are so often skewed in the media. According to international law we are the legal landowners of Israel. These facts serve to strengthen the ground on which we stand. I find it refreshing to read the time line and this well documented history. I am inspired by God's faithfulness and encouraged for the future by revisiting our recent past.

What is the Basis for the Legal Status of Israel and the Settlements?

Based on the writings of Professor Eliav Shochetman of the Hebrew University, Jerusalem.

1920 — The Biblical Bond Becomes a Legal Right

The right of the Jewish people over the Land of Israel (Eretz Yisrael) is based on the Biblical covenant between G-d and His people, and on the historical fact that this land was a Jewish kingdom till its destruction by the Roman Empire. From this time on the land was partly deserted, and no local entity ever emerged until the people of Israel started to gather from their exiles and revive their ancient homeland and Holy Land.

This Biblical right, founded in the book that cradles all Western civilization, was recognized in the modern history of international law. In 1920, after World War I had ended, the Allied Supreme Council that assembled at San Remo, Italy, decided, in accordance with the Balfour Declaration of November 2, 1917, to assign the mandate for the establishment of a national home for the Jewish people in Palestine to Great Britain.

This turned the right of the Jewish people over Eretz Israel into a right recognized by international law.

The historic bond that the Jewish people had with Eretz Israel consequently became a right legally recognized by the 52 members of the League of Nations. The United States joined the League at a later time, not having been a member of the international organization at the time. [and held a separate forum with identical final documents in 1925, establishing a homeland for the Jews in Palestine. -Shosh]

The significance of the recognition of the right of the Jewish people to Eretz Israel by international law was in its acknowledgment of the justice of the Jewish and Zionist claim to the land that had been stolen from the Jewish people by foreign occupiers and their right to have it restored to them. The recognition also voided the legal validity of the occupation of Eretz Israel by foreigners as well as the expulsion of Jews from it.

The Mandate over Palestine, which anchors the rights of the Jewish people to their country in international law, states that "No Palestine territory shall be ceded or leased to, or in any way placed under the control of, the Government of any foreign Power," and that "The Administration of Palestine . . . shall facilitate Jewish immigration under suitable conditions and shall encourage... close settlement by Jews on the land, including State lands and waste lands not required for public purposes."

The British government did not fulfill the aim of the Mandate where immigration and settlement were concerned (the decrees of the White Paper) in gross violation of its obligations under the Mandate. Additionally, it abused its role as the guardian of Eretz Israel for the purpose of the establishment of a national home for the Jewish people. In September 1922, just months after the confirmation in writing of the Mandate, Britain decided to separate the eastern bank of the Jordan from the western part and transfer control of the eastern side to the Arabs (Transjordan).

Subsequently, only western Eretz Israel — from the Mediterranean to the Jordan — the "West Bank" — remained, in the eyes of international law, as the area designated for the establishment of a national home for the Jewish people. It was this separation on which the peace treaty with Jordan was based, whereby Jordan kept the land on the eastern bank of the Jordan River and became the 'Palestinian homeland'. This separation specifically reserved the West Bank for Eretz Yisrael even as it gave the Eastern bank, which should ALSO have been part of Israel, away.

This legal status of this area — in the view of international law — has not changed to this day. Even the United Nations partition plan of 1947 was rejected by the Arab world, and on May 15, 1948, the day the British Mandate over Palestine ended, the Arabs attacked the newly born state with the express goal of annihilating it. It should be stressed that the partition plan was in fact no more than a recommendation, and had no power to bind the sides, and this too was, as stated, rejected by the entire Arab world and therefore became null and void in the eyes of international law. Judea and Samaria are part of the Jewish homeland.

Did the Jewish People Lose its Rights to Those Areas of Eretz Israel Lost in the War of Independence, 1948?

The answer to this question is no. Egypt did not establish sovereignty over the Gaza Strip and only two countries, Britain and Pakistan, recognized the sovereignty of Jordan over Judea and Samaria. In fact, Jordan never held legal sovereignty over the areas of Judea and Samaria, and has relinquished any claims to sovereignty there. The status and rights of Jordan over the parts of Eretz Israel it occupied for 19 years were at most the rights of an occupying force.

In consideration of the fact that Israel succeeded in restoring this territory in a war of defense that had been forced upon it, while Egypt and Jordan took the same territories by means of illegal aggression in the War of Independence, Israel's rights over the areas of Judea and Samaria take priority over the rights of the hostile Arab countries. These areas, therefore — from the point of view of international law — never ceased to be part of western Eretz Israel designated in its entirety for the establishment of a national home for the Jewish people, including of course, the right of Jews to settle in their land as established in the British Mandate.

Did the End of the British Mandate over Eretz Israel Generate Any Change in the Rights of the Jewish People Over its Land From the Point of View of International Law?

The answer to this question is also no. Article 80 of the UN charter was written to defend the validity of rights determined in the Mandate even after the mandate system no longer exited. After the areas of western Eretz Israel were liberated from the Arab occupier in the Six Day War (1967), returning them to the control of the Jewish people, all the obligations according to international law remained as they were. The purpose of these areas, after all, was that they serve as the basis for the establishment of a national home for the Jewish people.

It is in fact the duty of the Jewish state, which replaced the British Mandate, to fulfill these obligations. Israel's status in these territories, therefore, is in no way that of an occupying force, because in accordance with the outlook that has guided the State of Israel since its establishment, Israel does not annex territory that before 1948 was part of mandatory Eretz Israel. (i.e. Israel does not annex its own land)

Israel does not consider itself to have the status of an occupying force because it never considered the Arab countries that invaded Eretz Israel in May 1948 as having any sovereign rights over the territory of Eretz Israel they occupied. They were merely military occupiers. After this territory was restored to the control of the State of Israel, it became the obligation of the Jewish state — both from a Jewish Zionist standpoint as well as from the point of view of international law — to realize the rights of the Jewish people over the Western part of Eretz Israel in its entirety, including the right of settlement.

UN Resolution 242 Does Not Require a Return to the 1967 Borders

The media often refers to settlements and the presence of the IDF in the West Bank and Gaza as "illegal under international law." This is the Palestinian viewpoint, which is derived from their citation of UN Resolution 242, which states "the withdrawal of Israel's forces from territories occupied in the recent conflict [1967]." The authors of this resolution have stated publicly and repeatedly that they omitted the words "all territories occupied" and FURTHER, they added phraseology that called for "an accepted settlement" between the parties because "all States have the right to live within secure and recognized boundaries."

It is evident both from the paper reprinted today and UN Resolution 242 that Israel does INDEED have every right to sovereignty and settlement in the West Bank and/or Gaza.

The Geneva Convention Does Not Void the Mandate

This position, which views the right of Jewish settlement in Judea, Samaria, and Gaza as anchored in the rules of international law, is supported by a once-highly placed figure in the American administration, one of the drafters of the celebrated UN Resolution 242, a Deputy Secretary of State and professor of international law, Eugene Rostow. He wrote, "The primary objective of the Palestine Mandate was different [from the mandate over Arab countries]... The Allies established the Palestine Mandate in order to support the national liberation of 'the Jewish people' because of 'their historic connection to the land'. The mandate encouraged the Jews to found a national home in Palestine, and gave them the right to establish a 'National Home' in Palestine and granted them the right to make close settlements without prejudice to 'the civil rights and religious rights of the existing non-Jewish communities in Palestine'. The term 'civil rights' in this sentence is carefully distinguished from 'political rights.' "

"The right of the Jewish people to settle in Palestine has never been terminated for the West Bank... The only way which the mandate right of settlement in the West Bank can be brought to an end is through the annexation of the area by an existing state or by the creation of a new one." Rostow stresses that the right that arose by virtue of the Mandate is perpetual, as long as the territory of the Mandate is not turned into an independent state or does not become part of an existing one.

Therefore, from the point of view of international law, the recognized right of the Jewish people over all areas of western Eretz Israel is completely valid, including the right to settle throughout the territory.

Rostow also rejects the claim that the act of settlement violates article (49)6 of the Fourth Geneva Convention of 1949, which forbids an occupying power from deporting or transferring parts of its own civilian population into the territory it occupies. Professor Rostow writes that the settlers of Judea, Samaria, and Gaza were not transferred to live there as a result of deportation or "transfer." "The Jewish settlers in the West Bank are most emphatically volunteers," he writes. "They have not been 'deported' or 'transferred' to the area by the Government of Israel and their movement involves none of the atrocious purposes or harmful effects on the existing population that is the goal of the Geneva Convention to prevent [deportations for the purpose of extermination, slave labor, etc.]."

Furthermore, writes Professor Rostow, the Geneva Convention applies only to acts by one signatory country "carried out in the territory of another. The West Bank is not the territory of signatory power, but an unallocated part of the British Mandate. Even if the Geneva Convention could be interpreted as to prohibit acts of settlement during the period of occupation, it can in no way bring to an end the rights granted by the Mandate. It is hard, therefore, to see how even the most narrow and literal-minded reading of the Convention could make it apply to the process of Jewish settlement in the territory of the British Mandate west of the Jordan River."

And he continues, "But how can the Convention be deemed to apply to Jews who do have a right to settle in the territories under international law? — a legal right assured by treaty and specifically protected by Article 80 of the United Nations Charter, generally known as the 'Palestine Article.' The Jewish right of settlement in the area is equivalent in every way to the right of the existing population to live there."

Regarding the Geneva Convention, it should be pointed out that the willingness of the Government of Israel to recognize the validity of the Geneva Convention over the areas of Judea, Samaria, and Gaza was merely and exclusively for humanitarian reasons, and not for any other purpose. Judea, Samaria, and Gaza, on the other hand, are not part of any country and furthermore, from the point of view of international law, belong to the Jewish people.

Accordingly, the State of Israel — the state of the Jewish people — is entitled to declare sovereignty over the areas that according to international law belong to Israel. It certainly has the right to allow Jews to settle there, pursuant to international law.

Douglas Feith, who served as Deputy Assistant Secretary of Defense and Middle East specialist on the White House National Security Council staff during the Reagan administration, holds a clear view. He writes "[Although] the Mandate distinguished between Eastern and Western Palestine... it did not distinguish between the region of Judea and Samaria and the rest of Western Palestine. No event and no armistice or other international agreement has terminated the Mandate-recognized rights of the Jewish people, including settlement rights, in those portions of the Mandate territory that have yet to come under the sovereignty of any state. Those rights did not expire upon the demise of the League of Nations, the creation of the United

Nations, or the UN General Assembly's adoption of the 1947 UN Special Committee on Palestine plan for Western Palestine."

Feith explains that if the Jews do not have recognized legal rights to their claim to Judea and Samaria as part of their state, then they lack such rights in any part of Eretz Israel because all the rights derive from "the historical connection of the Jewish people with Palestine recognized in the Mandate."

He adds that the claim that the Jews do not have a legal claim to Judea and Samaria could be catastrophic concerning other claims the Jews have to sovereignty over Israel within its pre-1967 borders.

I have cited here only two experts in international law who hold this view, but the list of jurists and members of the administration who support the legality of Jewish settlement in Eretz Israel is very long and includes such names as Julius Stone, Professor Yehuda Blum and others.

Not only is the right of settlement in the Land of Israel an integral part of the Zionist vision — it is strongly anchored in the precepts of international law.